TO THE WOODS
A JOURNEY ALONG THE APPALACHIAN TRAIL

"I went to the woods because I wished to live deliberately, to front only the essential facts of life, and see if I could not learn what it had to teach, and not, when I came to die, discover that I had not lived."

FROM WALDEN BY
HENRY DAVID THOREAU (1817-1862)

Published 2020 by John Scott
First published 2004

ASIN: 1495426920

Copyright © John Scott 2020

The right of John Scott to be identified as the author of this work has been asserted by him in accordance with the Copyright, Designs and Patents Act 1988.

Apart from any use permitted under UK copyright law, this publication may only be reproduced, stored or transmitted, in any form, or by any means, with prior permission in writing from the author.

Cover design and typesetting by Raspberry Creative Type

Index

1	The Appalachian Trail	1
2	From Cowdenbeath to Atlanta	6
3	Georgia & North Carolina	18
4	Tennessee	68
5	Virginia	81
6	West Virginia	99
7	Maryland & Pennsylvania	109
8	New Jersey & New York	122
9	Connecticut & Massachusetts	146
10	Vermont & New Hampshire	154
11	Maine	165
12	Katahdin	193
13	Katahdin to Boston	205
14	London	211

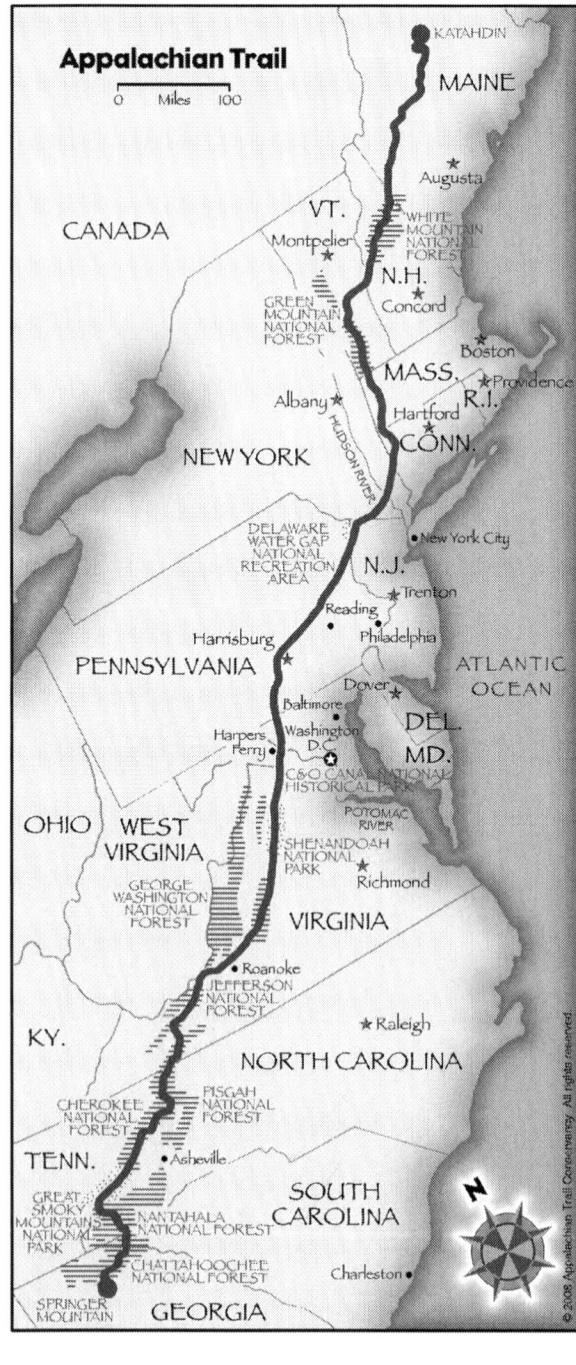

1
The Appalachian Trail

I hiked 2,100 miles to celebrate my life.

I started the Appalachian Trail at Springer Mountain, Georgia in April and ascended Mount Katahdin, Maine in October having hiked through fourteen states and three seasons.

That year, 2000, some 3,500 hikers intended to cover the route in four to six months, carrying all their belongings in a rucksack and sleeping in the forest along the Trail. Most 'thru-hikers' started in the early months and faced spring snow and storms, while others started as late as May and hiked hard to Katahdin to miss winter in Maine. The weather defined our lives for the length of the Trail, including start and finish. Like most, I travelled south to north, but a smaller number, known as south bounders or so-bos, travelled in the opposite direction.

About four hundred and fifty finished. Typical reasons for going home included exhaustion, lack of funds, boredom and physical injury or illness. In that millennium year the numbers of thru-hikers were the highest seen;

numbers have since dropped substantially, but the completion rate remains around twelve to fifteen per cent.

I first heard of the Trail during an extended stay in South Africa in 1995 when I had hiked no more than two hundred miles over a period of a few weeks, typically from town to town and comfort to comfort. The Trail is the oldest long-distance hiking route in the US and was begun with an article in the Journal of the American Institute of Architects on a proposed project in regional planning. Officials and volunteers took that project, or at least the route assumed by it, to something nearing completion in the period 1929-37 with a footpath over the Appalachian mountain range that stretched from Maine to Georgia. The Appalachian Trail Conference ("ATC") was formed at that time, charged with the management, promotion and protection of the Trail. The Conference remains a model of public/private cooperative management of natural and recreational resources.

A hurricane broke the Trail's continuity in 1938 and the effects of WWII and enforced rerouting kept it broken until 1951 when, yet again, much voluntary effort reopened it.

In 1968, the US Congress adopted the Trail as a unit of the national park system and the first national scenic trail, and created a means for state and federal bodies to acquire land. It is now the world's longest publicly owned footpath with much land around it also in public hands. Its upkeep is almost entirely conducted by thousands of volunteers in a federation of local outdoor clubs coordinated by the ATC, a small but highly effective charity based in Harper's Ferry, West Virginia.

I had no experience of hiking in the wilds, carrying my life on my back and being exposed to the elements over a long period. The challenges in my life had been academic and professional rather than physical and so I found it difficult to envisage this epic journey, in part because I could see no point in hiking such a distance. In a very real sense I had neither the tools nor experience with which to imagine the enormity of the Trail.

My faint-hearted approach to adventure combined neatly with a typically European response to American commercial and cultural imperialism. I imagined the Trail would be unimaginably long, lippy Americans would surround me, and it was likely to be sponsored by Nike, McDonald's and AMEX. 'Just do it, eat it and spend it' was not about to become the theme of my late thirties. My experience of travelling had always been in relatively comfortable places and cultures and it struck me as a piece of madness to attempt the Trail, which offered neither.

However, I later welcomed this very same madness into my life and I determined to complete the Trail to celebrate my fortieth year. Quite where my marked change of perspective came from was a puzzle to me, but I realised I wanted to do something that was significant, demanding and at a distance from home; to test my capacity for pushing mental and physical limits well beyond any point experienced to date; and to mark this keen moment in my life. The alternative of a party or a weekend break in Europe didn't excite me at all. Neither did my habit of ignoring my birthday and forgetting it was happening recommend itself to me. This year was different and I needed to confront the difference rather than scurry past.

The nature of my celebration was important and I wanted to mark the passing of my years with an activity that was increasingly inspiring and magical for me: to walk on the earth, through forests and over mountains.

From 1994 I had developed a passion for hiking which took me across England on the Coast to Coast route; to the French Pyrenees, and the pilgrimage route, Le Chemin de St Jacques; on countless inland and coastal trails in South Africa; and on short trips in Australia and Indonesia. Like most hikers, my interest started with day walks and then extended in both distance and time as I became used to completing a hike of two hundred miles every few years.

I liked feeling close to the earth and in a foreign country, being at a distance from home and not in a tourist spot. I liked moving around in a manner that was under my control and more natural than car or coach, giving me time to appreciate landscape and wildlife rather than rushing past and so providing an opportunity to slow my hectic life. Things happened when hiking that never happened when I was a tourist – I was more approachable and no longer protected by my status as a foreigner, so discussions with others were always easier and somehow more natural. I felt more open to whatever happened and I was up for anything.

There were other compelling reasons.

The millennium year with its promise of something special demanded commemoration of a different order. At Hogmanay or New Year I partied with abandon, eating black bun, a traditional rich fruit cake, and drinking fine malt whisky on a bridge across the River Thames in London before a long walk home. It was good, but not enough for a Scot who welcomed 1 January more than 25 December and who felt the passing of another year more than the festivities of Christmas.

The ATC marked its 75th anniversary in 2000 so there was great synchronicity around the year.

I had successfully completed three years of self-employment as a management consultant, helping clients integrate new businesses and develop their senior staff. I was working part-time, was paid well and enjoyed a balanced life, but felt I needed to change my comfortable status quo.

And I wanted to celebrate things American – in hiking over 2,100 miles I would discover more about this huge nation that had fascinated and appalled me since I was a boy. It was time to engage with the US in a continuing effort to understand both nation and people. The Trail would provide lots of opportunities to celebrate and engage as I hiked from south to north-east with Americans.

Even if the vast majority I would meet would be white, middle-class and detached from worldly interests, it would still be small-town stuff because the Trail passed close to the most densely populated parts of the nation, but through very few towns of any significant size. Americans had a way of describing this small-town experience – I would be hiking through East Bumfuck.

2
From Cowdenbeath to Atlanta

My teenage years in seventies' Scotland were crowded with things American.

The novels of Steinbeck, Hemingway and Scott Fitzgerald. The final paragraphs of The Great Gatsby still move me and Jay Gatsby remains a romantic hero.

The plays of Arthur Miller.

The music of Hendrix, Joplin and Jackson Browne, before the weirdness of Pere Ubu caught me and took me elsewhere. I liked the Sensational Alex Harvey Band, Stone the Crows and Nazareth, but they didn't quite compare. They lacked the 'otherness' of my US influences and spoke the same language as me. I was in thrall to the romance of dead US rock stars.

Pouting, sexy film stars like James Dean, Steve McQueen, Clint Eastwood and Marlon Brando. No women then or even now.

No poets, never any poets until William Carlos Williams some years later.

As a family, we watched the Fife Flyers play ice-hockey on a regular basis, warmed by sandwiches and coffee from a flask. And I played in the school basketball team, inspired by a TV series featuring the Harlem Globe Trotters.

I studied contemporary history at school in Cowdenbeath, a coal-mining community, and was immersed in some of the most potent political events of late twentieth-century America. I knew more about the US than I did about Scotland: the assassination of Kennedy, the Cuban missile crisis, the Bay of Pigs fiasco, Vietnam, the Berlin blockade and the Civil Rights movement all figured in my secondary-school education.

I wrote impassioned essays about black rights some years before I met a black person. I was enthusiastic about self-determination for Cuba and Vietnam long before I felt the same about Scotland. I argued the successes of the Russian Revolution in a schoolroom a few miles from a street named after Yuri Gagarin, the Soviet cosmonaut, in Lumphinnans, a town dubbed 'Little Moscow'. It was a profoundly international education that reflected a long tradition in Scotland of looking beyond national borders, although we were taught to look out rather than in.[1]

As a teenager, I thought of America as a modern nation at the cutting edge of technology, popular culture and twentieth-century progress. My cultural life and growing political awareness were greatly influenced by this huge, unknown country. I had a series of contradictory mental pictures involving unlimited personal opportunity

---

[1] Michael Lynch makes the same point in his Scotland

and immense suffering; huge wealth with grinding poverty; freedom of expression, but strict sometimes hypocritical social mores; great artistic and intellectual innovation and yet a profound anti-intellectualism.

I read novels, textbooks and newspapers to resolve this contradiction, this hugely stimulating puzzle somehow incapable of completion because pieces were missing or I just didn't understand the game itself.

In my late teens I was both fascinated and appalled by the country so perhaps it was time to visit and put to one side my obsession with study and hard work, forget my concern over lack of funds and conquer my nervousness about travel. But the work ethic was powerful in Scotland, where there was no tradition of gap years or taking time out after school and university and no tradition of young people exploring the world before committing to work and study. It was best therefore to work, given one had already enjoyed four years at university paid for by the taxpayer. The path available to me was education then work then retirement with whatever it offered to compensate for a life of long and solid effort. I didn't like the path, but was nervous about stepping away from it.

Reagan's election removed my fascination altogether. It was an entirely depressing time for those of us on the left in Europe, as we watched apparently unstoppable right-wing ideologues do their damage on both sides of the Atlantic.

The prospect of exploring this huge land that had influenced me so much was appalling, and became even more so as the US government intervened in Central and

Latin America and fuelled the nuclear-arms race. The first Bush government felt no different and all talk of compassionate conservatism was nonsense in the wake of a culture of greed and intolerance. He seemed to emerge from the bowels of the CIA and I didn't like what I saw.

Clinton's election was a time of great celebration, almost as much as when Mitterand was elected in France. And a three-week trip to the West Coast 1998 renewed my fascination with both nation and people.

On the flight to San Francisco via Chicago I saw acres upon acres of symmetrical farmland stretching to the horizon, with fields and farmhouses designed by a ruthless architect intent on detailed perfection and uniformity.

In celebration of my arrival in Yosemite National Park I raced to the top of the snow-covered Mount Hoffman, with its jagged peak of slabbed rock and rubble. Later the huge rock-face of El Capitan hovered above me as two tiny climbers hung in space with little to support them. Yosemite was a wonder of design that allowed me to hike away from a heaving mass of obese tourists to tranquil peace in less than fifteen minutes.

I visited Petaluma where in my imagination the ghost of Harry Partch still played his weird and wonderful instruments.

In Haight Ashbury I trawled through CD warehouses where I bought some Sinatra, arranged by a young Quincy Jones; Ben & Jerry's where I paid tribute to sixties' America with a Cherry Garcia; and a cigarette shop where

I found my favourite clove cigarettes from Indonesia. I experienced alternative consumption and celebration in a neighbourhood of which I had been in awe since discovering psychedelia some twenty years earlier. It was smaller, dirtier and seedier than I expected and my heroes were nowhere to be seen, apart from photos of Ben and Jerry, but I didn't care.

The US had impressed my teenage mind as a nation of cities, but towns and villages were more evocative of childhood interests and I expected to see John Boy Walton poking along Main Street. My childhood images of the country were confirmed: small towns had clapboard houses with porches, confusing road signs and diners serving huge portions. One house had life-size cut-outs of Monroe and Dean on display, otherwise it was empty and unoccupied. Perhaps a memory of those dead legends was enough to keep the house busy.

People I met along the way were to a person polite and helpful. We stopped at a breakfast fund-raiser for the local fire service en route from San Francisco to Seattle and left a few hours later having discussed President Clinton's travails with Monica, hiking in Scotland and malt whisky, and having been regaled with the ridiculous and the sublime over-easy, served with pancakes and maple syrup. I was surprised such an important facility was run by volunteers and funded by donations, but our hosts wouldn't have had it any other way. Public funding would be an imposition. It was my first experience of the independence of thought and action that characterised the nation, my first experience of public goods funded privately.

In Seattle's Tower Records the shop assistant was dressed in grunge gear, complete with tattoos and piercings. I asked him for his opinion on a Gillian Welch CD and he paused before replying that she played here recently, he didn't enjoy it, but was sure I would. While he politely suggested I was a sad old bastard, the disc he recommended was perfect and on it she sang like an angel, heart-stoppingly beautiful songs in a mountain twang with impossible harmonies.

I returned to London enthused and invigorated about my new-found relationship with the country. I saw immense space and great beauty where nature rather than man was the predominant force and its power was self-evident, more so than anything I had experienced elsewhere. I had reconnected to the culture which had influenced my teenage years so much. And I had met large numbers of Americans for the first time in my life.

Being there had pushed a button and there was no going back.

My preparations for hiking the Trail were limited and consisted of little more than attending a local gym to get fit. The instructor looked at me with surprise when I explained my purpose, but willingly devised an exercise programme. I attended every two days and quickly accepted that the conditions – it was boring, nobody conversed and loud dance music blared – were perfectly suited to the environment. Slabs of music with little if any melody got me on to rowing- and climbing-machines and drowned out any rational thought about the necessity of such misery. I had to see an osteopath to repair the damage done after my shoulder froze; I was in pain until he put me right within a few days of my flight to the US.

I plunged into a number of specialist shops in London with the briefest of instructions – give me gear that is light, idiot proof and functional. I wanted to hike and not be troubled by the capacity of my pack, mechanical efficiency of my stove or toggle value of my sleeping bag. I completed an excellent map-reading course, but never once had to use my compass and map on the Trail, so well was it marked.

I was unaware of the vast number of Trail publications, guides, websites and preparatory workshops available. Had I investigated any of them, I would have learned that the route I would be taking had seen various wars and that there were memorial stones to those lost in the War of Independence and the Civil War along the way, as well as a plaque to the WWII fighter pilot and film star Audie Murphy near the spot where his plane crashed in Virginia. I would have learned that the Trail evidenced the ebb and flow of industrial and religious development over generations, including coal in New Jersey, steel in Pennsylvania, forestry in Maine and Shaker communities in Connecticut.

I would also have learned that there are three main populations of thru-hikers: students who have left college or are taking a gap year; mavericks in mid life; and seniors. Held together by the Trail, their motives for hiking are varied. Individually they have different stories to tell, but common themes of challenge, reflection, celebration and discovery unite them.

Large numbers of thru-hikers spent months preparing dehydrated food and packing food boxes to be mailed to them along the route so they could eat relatively well and not be constrained by the opening hours and limited stock of local stores. Because of time and customs' constraints, I couldn't mail food in this way and so had to rely upon stores.

Instead of detailed preparations I focused on making money to pay for the experience and buy time to recover. I enjoyed a large degree of choice about when and how I worked, but the cost was that when I took holiday I didn't earn. In advance of this most demanding of experiences, my mind was on invoices, cash flow and tax returns.

Some degree of ignorance was a good thing. I did not want to be too well prepared and lose sight of the importance of luck and flexibility. I did not want too much understanding and insight because that would make me cautious again. In some sense my lack of preparation was the best form of preparation because anything else would quickly highlight the enormity of the challenge in front of me.

My Trail experience started in Georgia and so I flew south to hike north, to a state made famous in a Ray Charles song and remembered from schooldays as a bastion of slavery and racism. I felt I was flying into a very strange place.

The journey to Atlanta via Philadelphia was as unpleasant as only long flights can be: in-flight entertainment awful, vegetarian food a disgrace and space available for those of us over five foot minimal. I bought the cheapest possible ticket and got what I paid for.

It was all the more unpleasant because I had to deal with an immigration officer in Philadelphia – rude, racist if his treatment of other travellers was indicative, and not really prepared to believe me when I told him I was going to hike 2,100 miles. He asked me for a permanent address in the US. I didn't have one. During a long and trying day working in unnatural light, he found me a challenge to his procedures, fixed me with a steely eye and granted a six-month visa. Other foreign hikers were not so lucky and had to apply for extensions while on the Trail.

It was strange that a mongrel nation, which had clearly benefited so much from wave after wave of immigrants, could be so unwelcoming of others. Here was a nation neither short of space nor employment opportunities, and yet at that moment I was definitely in a foreign country, irrespective of visa, credit card, full documentation and passport. Awash in bureaucracy and surrounded by uniforms, all I wanted to do was hike.

The connecting flight to Atlanta was delayed; the plane, full of exhausted business people mainlined into their laptops and phones, sat there as rain bounced off the tarmac. This internal flight at the end of a day was a poor advert for working life because it conveyed a strong sense of work never ending, merely shading into countless hours of further effort. I started to feel a gap opening between these busy people, who up until yesterday had included me, and my new life in the woods. The next day I would be walking into a world about which I knew little and they would be working in one which I understood only too well. As I tried to relax my nerves jangled and my tummy wobbled.

So far the Philadelphia Sound was not very attractive and I didn't feel like shimmying across the tarmac to a 4/4 beat in bell-bottom trousers and platform shoes, surrounded by sweating bodies and bathed in disco lights. My expectations of the city, formed when my musical tastes included disco and soul, were confounded as teenage memories collided with adult reality. This sense of collision between a past measured in years and geographical distance and an immediate, direct experience was to remain with me throughout the Trail.

And yet . . .

I am blessed with being a Scot and having a Scottish accent, admittedly an anglicised one after years in London, and strangers always respond warmly to me whenever I am overseas. On the connecting flight to Atlanta I spoke with one of the flight crew. She was charming and helpful – yes I was Scottish, yes I did have family in the US, and no I wasn't sure if I was related to the kings of Scotland. When she heard I was doing the Trail, she offered to arrange free hotel accommodation in Atlanta if required. Would I like to borrow her phone to call ahead?

Such kindness, embarrassing in its generosity for buttoned-up Scots, would continue for a further six months. Though the nation was desperately insular and fiercely protective of its national boundaries, people would open their larders, homes and large cars to a stranger.

Hitching into a nearby Trail town would often lead to an invitation to stay for a meal or even for the night and it would take me time to realise that typical British reserve and a polite decline was inappropriate and almost rude.

I bumped into the air hostess again on a train from the airport to Atlanta. Her husband was a lawyer who had recently marked his professional success by leaving her for a younger woman. She was forging a new relationship and clearly enjoying the blossoming of a compelling experience, thinking about her future and determined to make it work. After a short train journey I knew more about that fine lady's life than I did about members of my family and old friends.

Americans talk about sticky and embarrassing things with little evident concern: this insight would strike me time and again. It is not a shallowness of thought and it isn't always poking their nose where it doesn't belong. It is a genuine interest in others – not just facts, but also emotions and feelings. They want to know and then want to know some more. People would walk up to me in diners, in towns and at Trailheads, where public roads intersect the Trail, and politely enquire if I was happy to answer a few questions. And then they would ask direct questions and look me in the eye – why was I not married; what did I really mean by doing the Trail to celebrate my fortieth; was I seeking to prove madness or merely get fit before my middle-aged body packed up; and wasn't this travel thing just a smokescreen for bigger issues?

It was a challenging experience as I felt my buttons pop and struggled to answer honestly, but it was also exhilarating and I very much enjoyed these conversations.

It was in those strange places and at unexpected times when I made contact with others. I felt as if there was nowhere else to be and the world around me disappeared. I touched perfect strangers and they touched me.

3
Georgia & North Carolina

I have finally reached the beginning of my journey. I struggle with jet lag and the arrangements to get away from Atlanta and so leave later than planned, travelling north from the city by mini-bus and cab. Both drivers tell me they hiked the Trail, but I see it in neither their faces nor their figures. The cab passes farmhouses and trailer parks, all of them surrounded by a clutter of rusting cars, and I talk and talk and talk in an effort to calm myself for the first day.

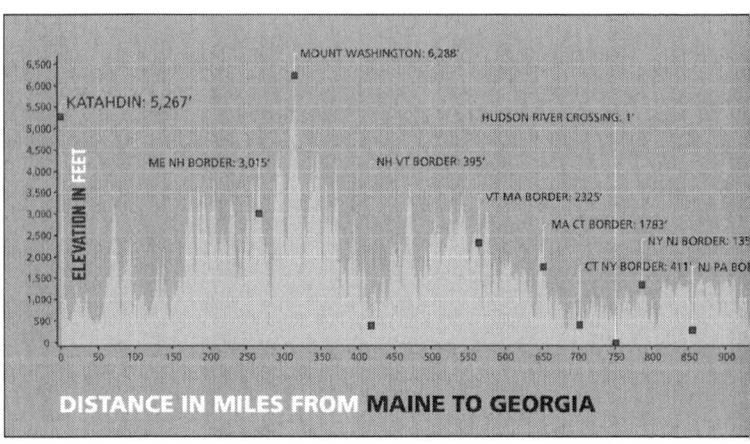

The approach route to Springer Mountain, the southern-most point of the Trail and the starting point, commences at Amicalola Falls State Park. I arrive at the attractive visitors' centre after lunch and change into hiking gear, leaving behind a pair of torn and fading Levi's, folding them carefully before I place them in the trash-can. Levi jeans have been with me for years so perhaps it is significant that I commemorate them in this way at the start of my new life, leaving behind an emblematic expression of America as I move into a physical one.

A stone arch marks my start. I wander along an elegant stone path which passes beneath it and then merges into earth. Tall trees and green bushes surround me and birds sing as I gaze along the track ahead which will ultimately stop in Maine. The mileage given on a signpost to Mount Katahdin, the ultimate finishing point, is understated, so often is the Trail relocated and extended to make it safer or more attractive for hikers. A fact of life is that it is never shortened.

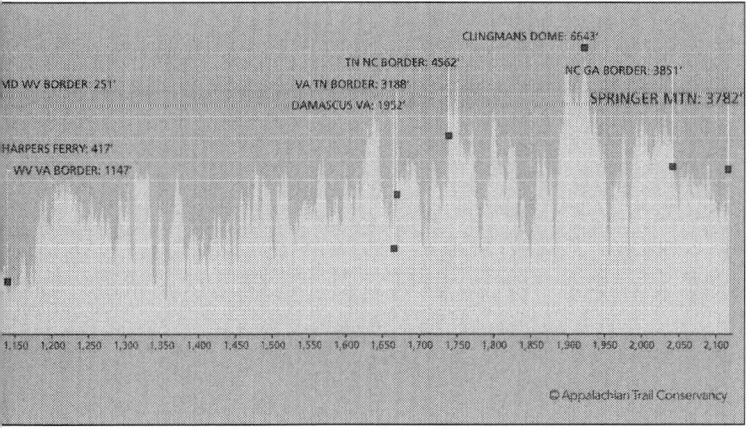

I am carrying everything I need on my back: tent, cooking stove and pot, sleeping bag and mat, pump to purify water, thermal and waterproof gear, and dehydrated food for the next four-to-seven-day period, during which I will be living in the woods before hitching to a nearby town to resupply. I have maps sufficient for the first 300 miles and the Appalachian Trail Data Book, which contains details of shelters, water sources and Trail towns and has an eye-catching photo of Katahdin on the front. At this point I am carrying too much and I will quickly learn to hike with less. I don't need two large bags of porridge oats, a pocketful of UK coins, two camping knives, several thermal tops and a detailed manual on Trail resources. My rucksack is relatively small, but it is packed to the brim and beyond.

I have chosen to start alone. I can't imagine walking with a stranger in an arrangement set up by phone or e-mail. It would be an awkward experience, obliging me to be on my best behaviour. Neither can I imagine walking with hiking friends, if only because none of them are available for such long-term madness. When I hike with others I do so at their pace, but this one is for me, an opportunity to see what I am capable of doing in terms of speed and distance.

The Trail is empty in early afternoon because most hikers commence in the morning. It will be months before I meet people who started the same day. I am excited and nervous as I slowly place one foot in front of the other, struggling to support a 45lb pack and knowing there is no way back apart from that marked 'Failure'. I feel I have made the right decision, but will only know after several hundred miles of testing both body and mind.

This is where it all begins, the point I have imagined for years and I am happy to celebrate my life and success in arriving here as part of a journey that has taken preparation and courage. I pace around the centre with a can of Coke in my hand, building up sufficient momentum to leave, and then with one final glance at the route back to Atlanta I plunge into the woods for six months.

The Trail runs along a ridge created by the Appalachian Mountain range, which comprises two great chains of mountain peaks separated by lowland valleys in the middle. Most of the Trail is covered by a green tunnel or enclosing forest so the claustrophobic feeling of being surrounded by trees is one that will grow familiar and feel prison-like. The fact that the first 500 miles are mountainous in the extreme will not diminish this feeling of being trapped by trees and landscape.

The Trail is marked with small vertical white paint blazes, one within sight of the next in areas where the path is not clearly visible or where others intersect, less often when the path is clear. Two blazes, one diagonally atop the other, indicate a change in direction to the left or right, although etiquette differs along the way. I can easily hike without maps so effective are the blazes, and when they disappear I stop and search for them, knowing I have wandered off and must retrace my steps. It is a simple and elegant means of marking my route through America, my route through my fortieth year.

After a few miles along this very steep path I meet a tall, gaunt man and his overweight partner who insist on taking my photograph while suggesting I won't make it to Katahdin. Other tourists gather round asking questions and I expect them to throw bananas at me. Later I meet a hiker who has been out for three days and is having problems with pack, tent and water pump. Indeed everything is going wrong so he's heading home. His shoulders slump, his eyes evidence confusion as his pack hangs awkwardly and he tries to convince me he will return at a later date. I am jet-lagged and nervous so my encounter with this saddened man increases my unease and I rest for a while on the side of a stream, literally shaking in anticipation of what is to come.

There are wooden, three-sided shelters every ten to twelve miles. Most are very basic, but some are large and more elaborate. They offer protection from the elements, proximity to a water source and a place to sleep for tired hikers. After a while I will avoid sleeping in them because they are open to bugs, extremes of weather and snorers. On my first night I sleep alone in the aptly named Black Gap Shelter, later discovering that most hikers aim for the next one because it is closer to Springer Mountain, our starting point. I hike down a steep side trail to pump water and scramble back just as mist drops to shroud the trees in a grey-white blanket.

My sleeping mat slips into a pocket of my sleeping bag, providing a base for the bag. When I am using it and sit up, the mat moves with me, hovering above and over my head. In the night forest noise disturbs me regularly, while resident mice run around my head and over my face. In the early hours of the morning I sit bolt upright, spooked by something near by; the forest is a noisy place at night and every noise might be a bear interested in a Scottish thru-hiker and his chocolate. I switch on my torch and look behind only to be scared witless by the mat hovering over me; if I'd had a gun, I would have blasted it. This feeling of being a city boy alone in the wild without the skills to deal with these experiences will be with me for months and miles. I feel ill at ease, a stranger in a very strange place, and fear invades my waking and sleeping moments.

Springer Mountain has served as the start of the Trail for those heading north since 1958, replacing Mount Oglethorpe to the south-west. There is a plaque marking the starting point, but I nearly miss it in my rush to get to Damascus, Virginia to meet my friend Robert, who will join me from the UK for a week's hiking in mid May. The original bronze plaque from Mount Oglethorpe is engraved with the words, 'A footpath for those who seek fellowship with the wilderness.' Unlike others, I don't take photos, sleep near the plaque or sign my name in the register along with a sentiment of significance. I am in a hurry and its symbolism is lost on me.

In the first few days, I endure a poisonous combination of fatigue and a diet of revolting dehydrated food. Mild hallucinations triggered by jet lag are normally entertaining, but in a forest they are threatening. I struggle to enjoy the dehydrated food, and although it fills a hole in my stomach, it never really provides a substitute for proper fresh food. All water for cooking or drinking needs to be treated with chemicals or boiled to kill any water-borne disease, so the very act of eating is tinged with a hint of danger and the occasional smell of chemicals. The basic human activities of walking and eating all present new and unpleasant challenges and little if any comfort.

My conversations with other hikers are about food, risks from wild animals and ill health, gear and miles – subjects about which I know little and care less. These days are not good ones as I settle into a new life that might last for weeks or months.

Over time these feelings will meld into something slightly more informed and accepting. I was never particularly interested in sports or outdoor activities, shunning them at school because I was hopeless and at university because my interests lay elsewhere. Here, I am in effect experiencing the challenge as a beginner. The sense of achievement at each day's end and anticipation of the next is both daunting and exciting, adding to a growing sum of miles and progress, both physical and psychological. Farther along the Trail I will hike with others who will push me towards long days of over twenty miles at speeds of three miles per hour, and I will be happy to travel these distances. I will start to know where my limits are and how to go beyond them, sometimes at a cost to my health. I will delight in this physical and mental challenge with new friends of like mind from whom I can learn a great deal. However, right at this very moment I am an absolute beginner.

On my second night I pull into Gooch Gap Shelter after a long hike in damp, misty weather. The shelter is signposted at 0.2 miles from the Trail – I will become used to this peculiar American practice of dividing miles – up a steep bank and shrouded in mist. At one moment I feel I have missed it or am lost but eventually I spot its outline in the gloom. The shelter is bursting beyond capacity with anxious hikers lined up like sardines in sleeping bags. I choose to sleep in my tent and start to erect it on stony, uneven ground. It's now I remember I have only done this once before, during sunny weather in north London on grass in the back garden.

The previous night in the empty shelter I struggled with my new stove until I realised it was upside down. This morning I turned a good breakfast cereal into sludge. This evening the learning is about setting up tents on stony ground. It is satisfying to master the technicalities of life in the woods: to discover what a good campsite looks like and how to erect a tent; to set up a stove in the dark and control its cooking speed while conserving fuel; to see where best to take water from a river or stream before purifying. The results of my learning pay off in everyday activities as I add to my knowledge and this makes me happy.

The next day I head off with hikers Lynda and Lewis for the outdoor-gear shop at Neels Gap where I am keen to make telephone contact with my family.

Lewis is a taxi-driver from Myrtle Beach, South Carolina and is escaping a job which in a twelve-month period involved a beating and an incident when he narrowly missed being shot in the head by a crack addict. This apart, he enjoys the variety of his job and the people he meets in a large tourist resort that attracts golfers from across the nation and beyond. He is medium sized, tanned and muscular and wears short-cropped hair that suits him perfectly. He is difficult to age in part because he looks so comfortable in his body: I guess late thirties, but he skilfully avoids answering the question. Lewis has what he describes as a taxi driver's belly, providing enough space for a cup of coffee and a burger to rest upon. His southern accent is musical and delivered through pursed lips and he and I struggle with our different versions of English – later I tell him that if we were to spend a day in a bar together I'd soon be pissed, only to see a glimmer of concern pass across his face. When I rephrase my statement, I discover that 'pissed' for him means angry. Lewis's sense of humour is dry and imaginative and he is good company at the end of a long day when he has groups of hikers in fits of laughter at his observations and anecdotes.

He has worked in outdoor activities, having broken horses and guided white-water ventures. Like a lot of Southerners, he has had experience of hunting and shooting in the wilds, usually with a number of uncles. This is his first experience of long-distance hiking so he is carrying far too much gear and struggles to manage a huge pack and tent. His hiking style is rather awkward as a result and he sways from side to side along the Trail.

He is separated from his wife, whom he describes as his 'ex-old lady', and daughter, but they figure a lot in his conversation and he clearly loves them both. There is a far-away look in his eyes when he wonders what his friends and colleagues are doing with his apartment and car. A sense of melancholy hovers over him at times.

Lynda is an interior designer from Brookline, Massachusetts and has negotiated time off after nine years with the same practice. She is small and delicate, but carries a pack that in the early stages seems to hover above her head as she moves along. She is careful and determined all at once, having prepared in detail by packing large food boxes with well-selected items, attending workshops and completing a number of outdoor trips. Her determination will allow her to deal with a painful hip ailment and still keep going, aided by an occasional visit to chiropractors and a well-developed sense of humour. The care she takes with her gear and diet sometimes shades into a slight obsession with detail – a trait every hiker evidences on occasion because it is all we have to protect ourselves from hardship. Unlike others, she looks smart and clean when hiking.

Her reputation for relatively expensive living, which will grow in the months ahead, is grounded in her belief that it's all right to suffer while hiking as long as you grasp opportunities for good food and fine accommodation whenever possible. Lynda's friends think she is crazy for hiking such a distance, but will support her with surprise gifts, invitations to visit and company while hiking, particularly in the later stages of the Trail in New England.

If I go over Blood Mountain, climbing to 4,400 feet, I might miss the shop and will bump into the five-hour time difference between here and the UK. Instead I skip around the mountain on a delightful side trail. Within the Trail community this isn't quite the thing to do – taking what is known as a 'blue blaze', or easier, more direct route. As a consequence some purists will claim I haven't hiked the entire Trail. Right now I don't give a shit because I want to call home and have a decent cup of coffee. I am relieved that having come so far I can be flexible in my approach and not too obsessive. It's one of a very small number of short cuts I will make and I relish them all with childish delight. Others insist on walking every inch from south to north, passing each white blaze on the way, but my life is way too short.

The route is difficult and made slippery by small streams, but the views are amazing. A huge cheese slicer has carved sections from the rock before scattering slices haphazardly across the mountain face. The mountain is surrounded by forest that stretches for miles and then shades into the sun-filled horizon.

I hit the shop on time and make my calls, happy to be in contact. I wander around in amazement at the luxuries set out in front of my eyes – fresh coffee, bread, cookies and a wide selection of gear. I have been in the woods for only three days, but it already feels like a long time.

Some ten per cent of those who start at Springer go home from the road on this Gap, or valley between two mountains. This is a frightening statistic: 300 people leave at the first road crossing after three to six days' hiking, having planned to complete the entire Trail. I struggle to understand why this happens and why people give up so quickly – dreaming is fine, but in my Presbyterian heart I know what matters is hard work and application.

What also matters is miles and time and I scribble calculations on maps and books in an obsession with measurements that won't disappear until I finish. Mount Katahdin may be 2,100 miles away, but after early October the chances of climbing it will be slim because snow and ice will be in abundance and make it a dangerous place. I have less than six months to complete the distance before then and a number of appointments to keep with hiking companions from the UK: as well as Robert in May, my friend Andrew will arrive in July and my partner Annie in August.

In order to keep my more pressing appointment with Robert in Damascus, Virginia I have to cover 455 miles in 33 days, a daily average of fourteen miles, involving seven to eight hours' hiking. The challenge is not impossible, but it assumes no rest and the weather may include snow, ice and driving rain. The terrain will be very difficult: there are a large number of mountains to hike over and significant elevation gain, which is hiker-speak for a deal of climbing up and down. Any fit person can do fourteen miles over difficult terrain, but the capacity to keep going day after day irrespective of weather is something else. I will need a combination of fitness, good luck and sheer bloody mindedness.

It is a significant test. At this early stage, not a day passes when my body doesn't talk to me in a loud and persistent voice. While at school and university, I worked for a construction company to which I was introduced by my friend Stuart. His Uncle Tom employed us and taught us how to deal with pain. Small accidents and minor injuries were common and his advice was to ignore the pain and it would go away. I wondered if this was just another way of maximising our work rate, but he was right. When my feet pound, shoulders throb and muscles scream at the beginning of another long day, Tom is with me. I try to work through the pain and discomfort, following his advice and the instructions of my osteopath, who provided stretching exercises that make me look like a very clumsy ballet dancer in hiking boots.

There is always a source of discomfort if not pain: a rucksack poorly packed or out of balance places extra pressure on my back; chafing occurs around my shoulders while my skin gets used to pack straps; I can't get my body temperature right as I move swiftly between being too cold and too hot; the internal frame of my rucksack digs into my back until I realise I need to carry it higher, thus making better use of various straps. Such discomforts will dog me for the first few months.

The footpaths in Georgia and North Carolina, the first two states on the Trail, are very demanding. The terrain is rugged in the extreme. I trip over boughs and rubble as my body becomes accustomed to hiking with a heavy pack and there is neither grace nor sophistication in my movements. My centre of balance is much higher as a result of my pack and I struggle to control it as I move along, awkward in large hiking boots.

The demands of the terrain are matched by the demands of my body. I do not sleep at all well. My digestive system is in revolt and appears to work only sporadically, a situation that will continue for the rest of the Trail. And my mind is in a spin because I am not at all comfortable in my own skin and my confidence is low. The luxuries of normal life subvert my thoughts on a regular basis and I am kept at my most obsessive, focusing only on the Trail, trying to discipline an undisciplined mind because to allow doubt would put me on the next plane home from Atlanta. This denial of doubt will remain with me to the end.

The ascents and descents of mountains are never made easier by switchbacks, zigzag paths that would soften the sting of vertical descents and provide comfort to knees and ankles as yet unused to such punishment. It's straight up one side and straight down the other. The Gaps or hollows that exist between mountains are no more than wind-blown accidents where descent from one mountain meets ascent of the next. It feels as though there is never any resting place.

There is a clear and brutal logic – I ascend, I descend and it hurts, the descent damaging weak knees and ankles carrying large loads. It is here where many start an ibuprofen habit, seeking relief from pain and inflammation and feeding a need that demands consumption well beyond recommended daily doses. The drug is so needed and popular it is known as 'Vitamin I'.

The Trail is exceptionally difficult, which helps to explain why many hike only five to ten miles a day. When they are in pain it is a great effort to put one foot in front of the other and I see hikers gingerly edge their way forward. One hiker I meet, Bernie, has pins in his legs as a result of a major motorbike accident that nearly killed him. He moves slowly and deliberately, supporting his large pack and damaged body with inordinate amounts of ibuprofen and food.

The Trail is by turns busy and quiet, and when quiet it is threatening until I become accustomed to life in the South. My city boy's imagination is too active out in the wilds. But who can resist the glorious trio of Big Cedar, Granny Top and Burnett Field mountains ranged over a four-mile stretch in Georgia? Where are the big cedars, what is granny's top and who or what is Burnett Field? Even the names of mountains are redolent of a not-so-distant and very practical past and only a fool would object to hiking when such linguistic delights are on offer.

In these early stages I talk to the mountains, thanking them for their kindness, but more often cursing and vowing they will not beat me. They are rugged and beautiful, set in a landscape that is spectacular in scale and colour. However, I experience each day as a battle and struggle against everything, but this is exhausting because the mountains are impossible to fight and will always win; I must try to relax into them and see what happens.

I move back and forth between matters practical and matters of the soul. Matters practical always take priority at the end of day:

- I camp where I like, except in national parks where rangers control sites. Typical selection criteria for a good spot include proximity to relatively clean water, shelter from the elements and distance from the road so locals don't visit.
- I set up my tent and ensure it is properly erected with sufficient tension on the outer shell to keep rain and snow off the inner shell. I lay out and inflate my sleeping mat, arrange my sleeping bag and liner along with whatever I use for a pillow and grab my torch before it gets dark because after that I am lost. The sleeping compartment must be kept secure so bugs and snakes can't get in.
- I change into something dry and comfortable and hang up damp clothes in the vain hope they will dry overnight.

A typical campsite

- I cook food on the camp stove, making sure the stove is properly put together and taken apart otherwise fuel will leak. I try to eat balanced meals with plenty of protein, fat and carbohydrates – but not so much as to run down supplies before the next town – otherwise I will be hiking while hungry and my body will run out of energy. Difficult hiking through challenging weather demands substantial amounts of food and it will be a while before I strike a balance between input and output.
- I clean cooking pots thoroughly at the end to reduce any chance of food poisoning.
- I purify a few litres of water for drinking during the night and in the morning.

- I gather together all food, toiletries and cooking implements in a waterproof bear bag of some description and find a strong branch fifteen feet from the ground and at least four feet from the trunk. I tie the bag with rope having thrown one end over the branch, weighted with a rock or smaller branch. I pull the bear bag to a height of at least ten feet and keep fingers crossed the bears don't get imaginative.
- I wrap my backpack in a waterproof cover and lean it against a tree.
- I brush my teeth if I can be bothered and use floss if I am interested in dental hygiene. I rarely am.
- I go to sleep not long after it gets dark because there is little else to do apart from read or write with a torch in my mouth and saliva dripping everywhere.

This will be the pattern of my evenings for six months.

After several days I rest at Goose Creek Cabins, have my clothes washed and sleep in a large bed after a hot shower. There is a pool-table in Reception, but it would be pushing boundaries too far to enjoy my rest in such a decadent fashion. For a few seconds I consider slipping into town towards civilisation, putting the Trail behind me for ever. I fall asleep giggling at the prospect of such an easy escape.

The next morning a hiker, Fennel, is effusive in her thanks to the lady owner and she replies in her musical Southern accent, 'Honey, would you like a hug?' – realising we are all strung out and far from home. This kind lady and her husband have been hosting large numbers of hikers this season; perhaps the wilderness experience is not going to be so empty after all.

The Trail rarely cuts through towns so when I need to resupply I hitchhike from Trailhead to town and then back. On this occasion I get a lift with Lynda and Lewis to the Trailhead, feeling clean and refreshed, ready for a steep climb away from the road on US19/129. Roads are usually logically numbered, but on this and other occasions there are multiple numbers to confuse hikers already confused.

I look at the map. Between Levelland and Cowrock Mountains at 3,800 feet there are four descents and five ascents in three miles. Boom, boom, boom. It's straight up and down as if those who designed the Trail sought to engage in a perverse form of natural selection. The elevation profile resembles a cross-section of sharks' teeth laid end to end, differing only in severity of possible bite. I flip over to review the northern half of the Chattahoochee National Forest and the teeth become bigger and sharper, with some descents almost vertical. I wonder at the geological violence that created this display, but don't have much time for wonderment as I struggle on.[2]

The map also makes clear I will hike in all directions over this section; I had assumed that hiking from south to north along a mountain ridge would only involve heading north. In reality the only direction I do not travel is west. It is perverse to be hiking over 2,100 miles and constantly to be heading off in the direction

---

2 The Eternal Frontier by Tim Flannery explains this geological phenomenon very well.

opposite to that which will take me home. This perversity grips me on occasion and I want to find whoever created this madness, seeking revenge for pain and discomfort by handing out a beating. Many months later I will meet Gizmo who takes time to explain I am the person who creates this madness. Shorter hikers point out I will be taking fewer steps compared to them and this provides comfort. And I will not be scampering around like a Trail dog, effectively doubling my mileage every day. I'm grateful I am not a short dog, but still angry.

There are hikers walking with dogs, fully intending to make it to the end. The owners organise mail drops of dried food to US Postal Service (USPS) offices and kennels outside national parks, where dogs are not allowed. A number of dogs are taken off the Trail with illness and exhaustion; unable to go on, they refuse to put one paw in front of another. One went home to rest only to die. Another finished in 1999 and was mown down by a car within weeks of climbing Katahdin. It is difficult to imagine the pain of losing a beloved pet that has provided companionship and comfort over months on the Trail. I feel comfortable with dogs around me and enjoy their company. The dogs are well looked after by their owners, benefit from special treatment and are greatly loved by us all. Trail Hound Outfitters in Asheville, North Carolina supplies dogs with backpacks, special treats, collapsible bowls, rain ponchos and hiking bootees. Only in America.

The nation's history as evidenced on the Trail starts to show itself. Near Tray Mountain on top of a ridge is the site of a dairy operated in the mid-1800s by a New

Englander. He produced an award-winning cheese for several years before common sense prevailed in this rather desolate spot. It is now a campsite with a spring where I pause for a snack and quiet reflection.

Tray Mountain is over 4,400 feet high and demands difficult climbing to get to a viewpoint. I arrive just before two hikers, Fried Bread and Tiny Little Animal, Tiny cursing in French and unembarrassed to discover I understand. She's in great pain and he's carrying a pack bigger than me from which he pulls a can of Coke. We laugh with relief as I sing part of the national anthem in thanks.

The view from the top is stunning – just miles of mountains and forests as far as the eye can see. It's Sunday when we summit and I wonder about the lives of people around the mountain getting ready for work the next day. When it gets dark I look for lights from surrounding towns and villages, but there are none because there is nobody and nothing out there. This is a very unfamiliar experience for me because it's difficult to have a sense of emptiness in the UK and parts of Europe.

The surrounding land is huge in perspective and empty of people and landmarks. There is a strong sense of being nowhere and completely unprotected and yet it is difficult to focus on this when I am so obsessed with making progress, eating properly and drinking enough water. But I enjoy this feeling of being out in the wilderness, carrying little to support my life there. My experience of Tray Mountain starts to convince me I can complete the Trail.

At Dicks Creek Gap on US76 I meet Cricket who is walking with two companions. They are having difficulty with huge packs and are in some discomfort. She however is in great shape and her boundless energy takes her up steep inclines in a few skips, long pigtails flying behind. I will see her again hundreds of miles later when her companions have left and she is busy attending weddings and celebrations. I also meet Brother, who is recovering from an attack of hives and has just enjoyed the luxury of an expensive motel room in nearby Hiawassee. I will see him again in Maine, twelve states later, where we take time to work out when first we met. This pattern of meeting hikers and then not seeing them for months will continue to the end.

I hitch into Hiawassee with a boat builder who has taken a loss in his day-trading account as a result of the recent collapse in dot.com values and IT stock. I burble about ridiculous valuations of invisible potential until I realise he has lost part of his pension. He is patient and trying to adopt a medium-term view, but right now he is clearly hurting. We scorch towards town and I jump out at an outfitter's to buy water-purifying tablets only to be told by the owner I am hiking too fast and his experience suggests I will not make it. He's a fisherman so I forgive him his ignorance.

Dinner that evening is my first experience of an All You Can Eat buffet where for a ridiculously low price I fill my belly to bursting with excellent food and soft drinks. Daniel's Steakhouse is busy and feels like a family enterprise where everybody knows everybody else and even local law-enforcement officers attend for an evening. I try iced tea with and without sugar and can't really escape the feeling it's just cold tea that needs heating.

Given the importance of tea to Scots and its role in shaping our daily lives, I believe there is something fundamentally wrong with the very idea of iced tea. I enjoy stewed apples, a dish of slow-cooked sweetened apples, sometimes spiced and served with savoury food. I try grits, coarse dried ground corn cooked with milk, eggs and butter, usually served at breakfast.

Lynda, Jorge and I are conspicuous for our hiking gear and lack of motorised transport – everybody else has travelled by car or pick-up to the diner. It's a farming community so diners leave early and the nearby supermarket is empty by mid-evening.

Next day on the Trail I sleep above its junction with the Chunky Gal Trail. In this post-modern, PC world it's difficult to imagine a hiking path with such a name and I work through various alternatives, including Fat Chick, Podgy Lady, Weight-Challenged Woman. All anticipated joys of Rainbow Springs Campground reduce when on arrival I meet Diamond Doug complaining bitterly about service and prices in language that would not be welcome in his legal practice. As I turn in towards Reception I see his point. Sign after sign tells me what I cannot do, but there is little to say what I can do. A hiker starts a monologue on the failings of my gear, hiking and diet before helping himself to a slice of my pizza, having advised that cheese for lunch is not a good idea. I like people with firm opinions, but I don't like him.

After spending large amounts of money on a few basic items and this over-cooked pizza in a smoke-filled store, I sneak into the restroom. If I understand the signs correctly (and it would take a good lawyer to express a view on them all), I am not a registered guest and therefore cannot use the facilities. Datto, whom I met the previous evening and with whom I will hike over the next few days, suggests if one Scot is allowed then we would all be at it, but at this moment I can't think of a better place for five million Scots to piss.

Datto works in IT to fund his trips around the world, and in spite of the chaos that seems to surround him, is exceptionally well organised and prepared. He experiments with various foods and offers me some disgusting supercharged high-energy goo, but compensates the next evening with a shot of Bailey's that he magics from the depths of his tall pack.

He is well connected in the Trail community and knows large numbers of hikers and volunteers. His on-line journal is well read and a number of readers make plans to meet him as he moves along; if there is such a thing as a Trail fan club, then he has one, because of his journal, good looks and easy smile. With people around him he seems distracted and semi-detached and then all of a sudden he focuses his attention on one of them and they connect.

That night the absolute fury of the weather is made clear. After a pleasantly warm day, the clouds open in the early hours and we are assailed with sheets of rain, gusting winds, pealing rolls of thunder and flashes of lightning. In a small one-person tent I am almost protected from the elements, but still can't find peace of mind to sleep. I fall out of my tent at 7 a.m. into a cold day. Rain returns and the temperature drops, by which time I am speeding along, but Datto perfects his habit of getting lost along the same piece of trail a number of times. This morning he does one hill at least twice before Lynda puts him right.

I stagger into Cold Spring Shelter cold and wet, seeking rest. It is full to bursting and beyond with damp, miserable hikers, some of whom are trying to inject a dark humour into our situation, but the shelter is so busy I cannot even find a small spot to sit a while. Before I become chilled to the point of hypothermia I move on, plunging into mist and rain for another six long miles to Wesser Bald Shelter, along the way passing tents secured against the elements.

Although there are no tree lines along the Southern Appalachians and few vantage points from which to view the surrounding landscape, there are Balds, large empty areas on top of hills and mountains. Their origins are a mystery: explanations range from the effect of harsh winters, snow and wind, through early attempts by American Indians to clear land for religious reasons, to the inevitable spacemen theories. In clear weather, they afford splendid 360-degree views, but today I see nothing as mist and rain envelop everything.

At the shelter Moxie is recovering from a close encounter with hypothermia, helped by Pat from Maine. He is cheery and offers a splendid pasta dish courtesy of Mrs Moxie, who supplies him with great food boxes from beginning to end. This shelter is also full, but it's too late for me to move on. I throw up my tent after this first day of bad weather and lie in my sleeping bag listening to planes overhead, realising I could be in one of them enjoying comfort and infinite amounts of dry clothes. It's my first experience of being wet, cold and sleeping out, and I have to face the prospect that tomorrow may be just the same. I have been told I would never laugh and cry as much as I would on the Trail. Tonight I do not laugh.

After a hike of seventeen miles in wind and driving rain it is easy to erect my tent quickly without thinking of location and without taking time to get the construction right. The result is a site that is terrible and I can barely scramble in and out because a tree is in the way. Pissing into a water bottle at 3 a.m. might be a useful learning experience, but a damp tent the next morning and a selection of damp clothes because I have jumped in and out during the storm remind me there are other ways to learn.

When hiking in the wild or moving around cities by foot, my sense of direction is good, though it is utterly hopeless when I am driving. Leaving camp the next morning I experience an absolute loss of this sense; not knowing whether to turn right or left, feelings of confusion, embarrassment and panic envelop me. The Trail looks much the same in both directions. I can't remember where I came from yesterday and in last night's mist there were no landmarks. Cursing my stupidity, I jog in both directions before getting map and compass out. Another hiker pulls past and recognises the symptoms, kindly pointing me north. We descend towards US19, discussing how quickly we adapt to the Trail and its rigours, but conscious of how much we have yet to learn.

On this Easter weekend I hear traffic from the road and smell the delights of cooked food before I see Nantahala Outdoor Centre (NOC) on the foaming Nantahala River. The centre was an early venture in providing outdoor activities and basic accommodation and is now a professional facility, owned by staff, with photos of pioneers scattered around restaurants and shops. They have a look of sixties' children who have taken their ideals and made them real in the seventies. Proper people enjoy their Easter vacation, eating and canoeing and biking. I feel different from them with their smart outdoor gear and they smell of soap and perfume.

At the store Lewis is waiting, having hitched from Hiawassee and sold his gear. He is leaving the Trail and I am saddened at the loss of an acquaintance who would have become a friend. His decision throws me, making me realise how easy it is to slip away without anybody noticing or caring, indifferent to the enormity of this move. I'm glad we have an opportunity to spend time together, toast our nascent friendship and mourn his decision to return to normal life.

Moxie opens a large food box from his wife and hands out dried apples from his backyard. I pass on the homemade moose jerky. Scott and Nora receive two twelve-ounce fruitcakes from Nora's mother who worries about them eating properly, forgetting they are hiking rather than driving and twenty-four ounces is a heavy load.

On long-distance hikes I usually become squeamish about food, and ill disciplined about drinking water so I quickly lose weight. In anticipation of this, I tried to put on weight before the Trail, but with little success. This time is no different and my weight loss is substantial and swift. I am trying to eat three times a day and snack in between to regain lost weight. My body is starting to change shape as muscles develop in legs, arms and hips where the majority of my pack weight is carried. I look lean and muscular which is a good feeling after three years of relative sloth and generous eating. Towards the end of the Trail another change will take place when my leg and arm muscles become more defined and excess fat disappears. I like my new shape, but worry about how much effort I can sustain and fear I am using more energy than I am producing. I am in deficit to my body and the means of making good this deficit is not available to me. Fortunately the human body is capable of taking much more punishment than we usually deliver to it in our comfortable lives.

Lewis and I eat lunch before I shop for food, liquid fuel for my stove, some small items of gear and a watch. I thought I might get by without reference to time and dates and without need of an alarm, but I cannot. I need help to wake in the morning and measure progress on an hourly basis so I can get to a good sleeping spot before dark and keep on track for Damascus.

A fact of life on the Trail is the gear thing, completely unavoidable and yet utterly boring. What is painful in the early months is the multiplicity of gear discussions. I carry a Swedish tent only now being distributed in the US so inevitably get caught in long debates. On my second day I shared a shelter over lunch with a number of hikers including a young woman and a group of men. The men talked gear in detail, celebrating the recent release of a titanium stove from a well-known manufacturer, and almost climaxed in unison when they saw my tent although it never really has that effect on me.

Gear geeks are strange animals and I am not one of them.

Nevertheless some of us are obsessives and obsessing publicly is a good thing, helping us to manage the demands of the Trail. If we all suffer together, some individual suffering subsides. As large numbers of us get used to hiking gear, sometimes for the first time, it helps to talk and work things through. Indeed we all became experts and learn that there is some distance between manufacturers' claims and reality. My pack proves to be barely showerproof and the pack cover provided by the same manufacturer not waterproof. This will become very relevant farther along when I get soaked on a freezing day in the Smokies. If I only have two T-shirts to wear in six months, I need to know they will withstand a lot and not smell like a badger's bum within a few weeks. In fact my T-shirts will see me to the end, but my trail shoes fail the badger test very quickly.

Large numbers of us were poorly advised or even ripped off by outfitters – Jorge has a LARGE pack when it is evident to anybody he is a small man. An outfitter thirty miles from Springer Mountain does a roaring trade in helping hikers ship their useless gear home and re-equip with more appropriate gear. One has brought a hiking chair while another is carrying a barometer. USPS must welcome the thru-hiking season when they make good money from returning unwanted items.

With clean, warm clothes from the laundry and a cold beer from a Trail Angel I head to the bunkrooms to dry my tent. Angels are to be found along the Trail, local volunteers active in the community who provide help, advice and little treats or Trail Magic, one more example of the hospitality afforded to strangers. They are very real angels on many occasions, passing along emergency messages to hikers and shuttling them back and forth to doctors.

On a Saturday evening in late April a number of us gather in a restaurant at NOC for dinner. The food is excellent, venue perfect and we are well looked after by a crew who know we are on the Trail. I feel the care and attention given to us and it lifts me.

I also feel bonds developing as we celebrate a hundred and thirty miles together. There are conversations about home life as we spin into fantasies about hot showers and warm beds. We make detailed examinations of the menu and discuss what delight is next, calculating how much of it can be wrapped for tomorrow. Over time we will become experts in packing fresh food in Ziploc food bags and camp pots to supplement dehydrated food in the first few days after leaving town.

And there are hilarious exchanges about the many mistakes so far. Falls are a common occurrence as hikers get used to big boots, walking poles and heavy packs. Some end up in positions from which they cannot exit and depend on the next hiker to extract them, hopefully without photographic evidence. I typically go head over heels on perfectly flat ground and into mud.

I have read a significant amount of research on what makes a group function well and I suspect we fit most of it – shared common purpose, clear goals, mutual respect, a variety of useful and complementary skills, frank exchange of views, willingness to support and help. Leaderless of course, but we don't need leading. I start to feel as though I belong with these people. We are in this together and our identity drives us on.

I feel some regret at leaving Lynda and Lewis behind, Lewis to make his way home for October when his taxi and apartment become available and Lynda to tend a painful hip. I know I will find a way of keeping in contact with these people whom I met within a few days of starting. It has been this way for me since school – the bonds formed at the outset remain the most powerful, irrespective of whether subsequent contact is frequent or only occasional. The initial nervous exchange, the sharing of a new experience in its early stages and passing through it together form a bond that is difficult to break.

The next morning it rains and blows, reminding me of any English public holiday. The climb away from NOC is steep and muddy, made worse by rain and wind that is now gusting. As I hit the ridge, the wind almost lifts and carries me off. I struggle to get into waterproof gear, but it's too late; I'm soaked and in danger of now soaking two sets of clothes. I charge past an elderly hiker and pause to return his watch to him, found farther back. He is immaculately dressed in smart matching gear. I will see him again some 870 miles further along, heading north out of Harper's Ferry, West Virginia. He will be just as smart, but his clothes will be hanging off him because he will have lost so much weight. He will proudly remind me of the return of his watch.

I run into Sassafras Gap Shelter to rest awhile and wait for the storm to pass; sheets of water are being driven before a furious wind. Fennel follows me and needs help to remove soaking clothes before cooking a hot meal and she shivers as I peel gloves from her frozen hands. Hypothermia strikes quickly and can kill in the strangest circumstances – an unwelcome, silent companion when weather is foul.

The next day, while resting in the Fontana Dam Resort, I reflect with Breck on the challenges ahead in the Great Smoky Mountains National Park: the likelihood of poor weather, given that even in April it can snow; Clingmans Dome, at over 6,600 feet the highest point on the Trail; an abundance of regulations policed by rangers whose reputations go before them; busy shelters which we are obliged to use, with bear bars on the entrances so that we are imprisoned overnight; footpaths trashed by horses and hogs; a park blighted by acid rain, pollution and disease. I am putting in long miles every day and will soon reach an average of twenty so the prospect of the park is not an encouraging one because I will have to deal with its challenges when tired and strung out.

The resort offers cheap off-peak accommodation to hikers and fishermen. I sleep here after two days of wet, cold weather to gather myself for the Smokies – drying my tent over a bath, diving into an all-you-can-eat buffet and going back for more the next morning, mailing unwanted items home.

Fontana Dam was built at the southern boundary of the Great Smoky Mountains along with this huge camp to house construction staff and their families. In a country oblivious to irony, the conversion of accommodation for this heaviest of industries to a late-twentieth-century tourist resort goes unremarked. The dam is well engineered, showing its age somewhat in beautiful surroundings. No doubt there were bitter struggles when the Tennessee Valley Authority sequestrated land for the project and even now decades later families object to the TVA's activities.

Checking out, I see a school photograph with ranks of children beaming at the camera. The dam and its construction shaped these children's lives and I wonder about this strange experience. What was it like to live as part of a massive construction effort and where did these children go when it was all finished? Was it a one-off experience or did their fathers chase work around this vast country, exposed to the vagaries of boom and bust that are expressed so sharply in the construction business? How many children were left without a father as a result of fatal accidents?

Americans love reunions – hikers regularly get off the Trail for family or college gatherings, huge affairs where hundreds of people attend. I wonder if these children meet even now.

As I stride across the dam in sunny weather an elderly gentleman with a long, flowing grey beard wanders down the steep hill towards me. He is a volunteer who looks after this part of the Trail and ensures the first shelter is in good shape. My accent sends him into a detailed account of the number of foreigners in the park this year and he cheers me with his knowledge and commitment.

From the dam I charge with Otter and Diamond Doug towards the fire tower on top of Shuckstack Mountain, gingerly climbing up to the cabin high on its shaky wooden supports.

Before satellites and the easy availability of helicopters, fire towers were the sole means of fire watching in many parts of the US, the sole means of pre-empting an event that can be physically and economically disastrous. Norman McLean's Young Men and Fire vividly describes how fire fighters were parachuted into key areas, equipped with only basic tools, to dig trenches and cut trees in an attempt to contain ravenous blazes.

The views are stunning, but there is a haze over the park, visible evidence of pollution. Large swathes of trees are dead or dying, their unnatural colouring a painful reminder of the damage we do by indulging in excessive consumption. Some damage is pest related, but trees, conifers included, are weakened by pollution. Viewing the devastation from the top of the fire tower is a humbling and deeply worrying experience.

Otter interrupts my pessimism with a reminder that there are between four and six hundred bears resident in the park and our packs are some distance away. Bears have a keen sense of smell, good appetite and powerful claws, all of which constitute a threat to hikers' packs. We leave Doug to complete his on-line journal and scurry off.

Diamond Doug is a lawyer who hikes with a flask of malt whisky and a supply of clean casual shirts to don before late-afternoon snacks of crackers, cheese and sausage. I take to him immediately when I discover his taste in whisky, but pause a moment after discovering he also uses ice, which for many Scots is close to sin. He maintains his meticulous approach to dress and food along the Trail and he struggles to understand why others can't be as well organised as he is.

Doug is tall and good-looking and his angular body carries little extra weight. His eyes burn with enthusiasm and passion and he knows, really knows, he will complete the Trail. In another life he would have been a preacher. He displays a number of the traits common to those of his profession – a capacity to argue about minutiae, strong views on a variety of topics, a desire to give advice on matters varied, and a very rational approach to issues that don't always lend themselves to rational analysis. His on-line journal includes a detailed argument on the pros and cons of slack-packing, or travelling without a backpack.

Doug has a facility with words that he displays in shelter registers and he participates in debates whenever the opportunity presents. In amongst all the words he is excellent company and there are occasions when his unbounded energy helps me move along.

That night Otter and I share a shelter in the Smokies where two hikers from Florida keep their radio on. I fall in and out of sleep to classic rock music; it reminds me of listening to Radio Forth when I was a teenager. 'Been a long time since the rock 'n' roll.' I look at the Floridian hikers, think of Carl Hiassen's books and resist asking them to switch it off. And we are still in Deliverance country.

I meet my first foreigner in this shelter. Digger is an Australian postman who is having serious problems with his knees and only has until mid-September to complete the Trail. He's swallowing as much ibuprofen as he is M&Ms.

A young ranger with a huge gun calls in to pay his respects. He's off to get him some hogs, but barely looks old enough to carry a pencil let alone a gun. I never see hogs, but I do see evidence of their activities where they have dug into paths with their sharp tusks. Farther along the Trail I will meet Kent who tells me he slept out with his wife in the park some years ago and woke to discover hogs had been digging around them. Hogs take no prisoners when protecting their offspring and food so they were lucky not to have been attacked. On another evening in a shelter a number of skunks tried to join his daughters through a hole in the flooring. Needless to say his family are less keen on the outdoor life than he is.

I wake in the morning and take my pack outside. A mouse dances around me as a deer ambles past, neither knowing nor caring about my presence. The deer captivates me with her ineffable grace until I sense Otter ready to go. The dancing mouse is worrying about her newborn children who are inside my pack in a nest made from two thermal tops. She climbed in overnight, although my pack was closed and hanging from a nail above the entrance to the shelter, chomped my tops and made a nest before giving birth. This puts my belief in animal rights to the test and I want to stomp on them. A look from Otter and some quiet reflection stops me and I put them in a basin from where Mom collects while Pa hovers inside the shelter. Their descendants will now be preparing for the next thru-hiker season.

After the 2,000-foot climb to Shuckstack, the elevation gains are not so significant, but it is still a steady incline to Clingmans Dome, more akin to hiking I have done elsewhere in the world. I relax and benefit from Otter's knowledge as a field biologist and experienced long-distance hiker. The animal and bird life is magnificent, although I only observe at a distance as an amateur. I know little about wildlife and it shames me as Otter identifies spoor, birdcalls and animal tracks before completing his journal at the end of day, listing everything he has seen and heard.

It's in the Smokies that I hear ruffed grouse. When the male beats its wings the sound is like a generator starting up – boomph, boomph, boomph, boomph. This is very disconcerting for somebody who has never heard it before and has me puzzling why there are generators in the woods. It's also a worrying experience when the 'beat' of the generator coincides with my heartbeat, as though it is racing out of control. The female protects her young by limping to distract our attention from a nearby nest. If this doesn't work, she then attacks with vigour. I start to recognise this tactic in a number of animals and birds, as adult females make themselves too visible and available.

Wild turkeys look, sound and fly as though they have been supping bourbon of the same name. There is no grace to them and what they lack in subtlety they compensate for in their joyous, life-affirming noisy presence. Their call is a combination of scream and manic laugh, blousy old things no longer caring what their public thinks of them. Clumsy when they waddle, they are even clumsier when they fly, crashing through bush and undergrowth on their way towards the light, leaving behind a terrified hiker wondering what size of beast has rushed past him. The aged bourbon is of a much higher quality, although I am careful with such talk, given I am in the wrong state to praise Wild Turkey, which is distilled in a neighbouring state, and my thoughts on the local Jack Daniels do not bear repeating.

Views from the park with the ribbon of Fontana Lake to one side and immense flatlands of Tennessee to the other are breathtaking, sometimes literally so at times of the year when ozone levels are high. The diversity presented to us is arresting even for an amateur – in its richness it feels and looks different from the previous 160 miles because for the first time I can see around me, having emerged at last from the green tunnel. I feel free of the forest that has enveloped me for over two weeks and the landscape is more varied as the seasons turn, edging slowly towards summer.

I see heathers and gorse that remind me of Scotland, an immense number of birds, compensating for their absence elsewhere on the Trail, and wildlife in abundance, including deer that appear from nowhere to entertain us. In the park there are more than 100 species of trees, 1,500 flowering plants and 2,000 varieties of mushroom. I sense an explosion of activity around me, some of it hidden and silent, making its presence known in various ways – lives are being lived as Otter and I skip and stagger along the Trail.

The Observatory on Clingmans Dome, a concrete spiralling edifice, stands as an insult to the beauty of the landscape around it. Otter braves the crowds and his pale gaunt figure stands out among the serried ranks of overweight, over-dressed Americans moving around in ever shifting hordes. Again I smell soap, clothes detergent and perfume. A group of teenagers gather around as we move out, clamouring to ask questions, unsure how to treat these strangers doing strange things. Five minutes after leaving the Observatory we have left the crowds behind; it is as if there is a barrier beyond which they cannot go lest they stray from transport and park facilities.

Otter is a contained explosion of energy in a small wiry body topped by a shock of hair that is out of control, an absolute hiking machine. He is seeking to complete the Trail in four months and return to his parents and girlfriend. On occasion he seems torn between his desire to hike and a deep longing for home.

He talks at speed and hikes at speed and whenever I see him I rush to catch up with him, irrespective of what he is doing. Conversations are high-adrenalin, roller-coaster experiences as we move from topic to topic. He has strong views on a number of subjects, but in amongst his speed of delivery and range of topics he is always mindful of different perspectives.

His gear is in a state of disrepair and he hikes with trainers that are likely to fall apart at any time. His pack is out of balance and his tent looks as though it will be blown away. If Otter slowed down, people would want to cuddle him because he looks so vulnerable. But this outward appearance disguises an orderly mind that ensures he carries only what he needs at minimum cost. Amid this apparent disorder there is careful planning and a frightening degree of focus. And yet he is also charming and considerate, taking time in the Smokies to talk to me about eating properly and giving excellent advice on chafing.

I spend less than four days with him, but the experience marks me for the rest of the Trail. Never before have I met anybody who lives life at such speed.

We stop at Mount Collins Shelter where there is space to sleep and move around. The night is cold and we are at 5,900 feet, but Otter throws up his tent. I nearly set my stove on fire, having primed the burner too generously – fuel is pressurised in the fuel bottle before it is released to the stove, making a hugely efficient Molotov cocktail encased in reinforced metal. I have already heard the story of a hiker who burned down a shelter with an exploding stove.

The next morning we wake to snow and ice. One hiker has had enough and is leaving. Having had doubts since Springer Mountain, he promised he would hike to Clingmans Dome and there conclude his Trail experience. I shake his hand, wish him well and congratulate him on his brave decision. It is rare for hikers to announce they are leaving; most choose instead to slip away quietly and it always saddens me, irrespective of whether I know them. We leave behind a solemn shelter with various hikers heading into nearby Gatlinburg, some never to return, with one looking desperately lost and unhappy in the snow.

I meet a German hiker heading south after an evening spent with a companion who collapsed into a diabetic coma and was carried out by rangers on horseback. There isn't much sympathy for this ill man from his companion or others I meet later in the day, given he had been careless with his diet. Hikers are supportive in the most demanding of situations, but withering when people take unwarranted risks with their health or that of others. The Trail doesn't allow for much leeway on matters of health and well-being.

Melting snow turns the path into a deep mud bath and I am careful where and how I place my boots. But thick leather, serious waterproofing and thermal socks fail to protect my feet and they soon lose sensation. The trees shed their wet, icy loads over me so I am assailed from all directions, and the temperature increases only slightly as I drop rapidly down the mountainside on to Newfound Gap, the one road crossing in the Smokies, to provide entertainment for coachloads of tourists. My hands are so cold I have to warm them for a few minutes before I can piss.

That night I pull into a cold, grey camp and stagger into a busy shelter where Walkin' Home makes introductions and finds sleeping space for me on a bunk. He can see I'm tired and stretched, and takes time to chat after supper. We will meet again near Davenport Gap and then in Hot Springs. We have little in common apart from a sparkle in our eyes, common decency towards others and a willingness to debate and argue, but we enjoy spending time. We will never get the chance to hike together and that is a regret. In my photo of us relaxing at Elmer's in Hot Springs, North Carolina a sense of conversation and experience waiting to begin is palpable. I anticipate our next meeting with great enthusiasm and know it will be worthwhile when it happens. There is a community of hikers out there, held together by the shared experience of hiking thousands of miles and always ready to re-establish old bonds when opportunity presents.

Otter and I speed along in difficult weather over challenging terrain. I now know I am capable of pushing myself beyond that limit which has been in place for some years and I break it on a daily basis. We pull out of the park late morning having completed 71 miles in less than four days. My feet are cracked and bruised, but everything else is in good shape. I celebrate with a huge lunch, huge dinner and supper of ice cream and soda at Mountain Mama's. Otter takes off, intent on doing another four or five miles before the day is out and I never see him again.

The diner offers accommodation in small bunkhouses. At ten dollars it sounds a bargain, but the place is so dirty even ten dollars is a lot. The owners are contemptuous of hikers and local health officials are too busy to close both bunkhouse and kitchen. There is nothing else on offer so, weary after days of hard hiking, I choose to stay.

I walk into a bunkhouse to find somebody there already, dressed in battle fatigues. In the UK those who wear battle fatigues are almost invariably harmless. In the US they might very well be dangerous. The freedom to carry guns is what makes the difference.

The young man wants to impress a number of things upon me. He has weapons and enough food for three months buried in the woods, and enjoys going into the woods under cover to observe hikers without their knowledge. His flick knife is just within legal limits and he flicks it open to show me, pointing out its finely sharpened edge. He is proud of his daughter who can field strip a rifle and knows how to use a grenade. She is also skilled in self-defence and has recently beaten a relative who is bullying her – this much I appreciate. His estranged wife complains about him turning up at her house dressed in battle gear. His gun collection is significant and he enthuses about make, power and preferred ammunition.

Later in the evening he opines that all US liberals and homosexuals should be shipped to Europe. I am lucky in having Walkin' Home as a companion that night: he is an ex-member of the US Special Forces and handles the young man well. As Walkin' puts it the next day, the young man has left the army, but the army hasn't left him. He is without an identity and purpose, pursuing his dreams on the fringes of life.

He would have been really frightening, but when he menions that his mother is coming to collect him in a few days my picture of a right-wing fundamentalist survivalist changes somewhat. I will see him in a town some thirty miles farther along, when he greets me as his Scottish friend – he knows he was out of order and seeks to make amends, but I can't quite respond to his offering. It is one of the rare occasions when I am glad I am not from round here.

He is a good example of a strain of thought in US politics – it can be found very easily on the Web and in publications and I sensed it just below the surface of a number of conversations I had with locals. It is profoundly racist and homophobic, completely distrustful of officialdom, opposes any form of federal influence, especially in relation to gun control, and worships the principles of personal choice and freedom of political belief. What matters is that people will suffer and die for their beliefs. Should these ultra-right-wing organisations and groupings ever manage to act in concert, it will be time to worry. Walkin' and I shrug our shoulders, confident in the knowledge that it won't happen, choosing to forget that it continues to happen in many parts of the world.

The gun thing frightens me.

Before heading to Springer Mountain I stayed with Bill and Judith in Atlanta. Bill mentioned in passing that in New York it was all right to shake a fist or two at other drivers. To do this in Atlanta would get you shot, he warned, and I believed him. I will be reminded of his words some sixty miles out of Washington DC, when Dave refuses to stop for somebody flashing his lights at him because the other driver might be carrying a gun. When I arrived in the US, some kids had settled an argument in a public zoo with a gun and paid the price of adult folly.

I have never understood the logic of arming citizens when so much mayhem results – children are shot in accidents at home, school grounds become killing-fields and simple human transactions are skewed by an ever-present threat. I find the constitutional-right argument perverse in the extreme, given it was prepared when the US was without a standing army and the only arms available to most were farm and garden implements; those who drafted the Constitution could have had no concept of how things would stand in their country in the late twentieth and early twenty-first centuries.

The response to gun-related tragedy and slaughter in the US amounts to a shrug of the shoulders on the part of lawmakers, ridiculous justifications from the National Rifle Association and a singular lack of public interest apart from token hand-wringing. When action is taken, it's usually by mothers desperate to point out the effect of this madness upon their children.

I want to believe the US is in the process of maturing as a country and a democracy – countries take time, for example, to extend the vote and ban capital punishment, so perhaps the US is coming to terms with the evils of weaponry. But farther along the Trail I will see Charlton Heston spewing his poison on behalf of the NRA during the 2000 presidential campaign, when the organisation spends millions of dollars campaigning against the Democrats. I will see racks of rifles in pick-up trucks and know things will not change. And I will see the First Lady saying on television that she supports the constitutional right to carry arms, but wants to put locks on triggers and introduce minimal controls at the time of purchase.

I will get a lift from a man in Maryland who bemoans the death of a child in a domestic accident in which two children were playing with their father's gun; one is now dead and the other must grow up with the knowledge of what happened. Even the language of reporting is perverse: it is not an 'accident' but a tragedy that a young life has been snuffed out by a weapon of destruction. I expect the man to condemn the situation; instead he talks of tighter controls and trigger locks.

This is playing around at the edges, putting metaphorical sticking plaster on gaping wounds. It is strange fruit of a different order, a matter beyond debate and discussion.

It is in North Carolina that I am at my most tearful, for reasons that are utterly unclear to me, in part because I rarely experience this most necessary of human responses. Perhaps I am strung out and tired as the Trail takes its toll. Perhaps it is the poignancy of early spring as I pound along an undulating path through banks of blossom, shining white and rich in perfume. Perhaps I now feel a great distance from home as I become more aware of my situation and less obsessed with practicalities.

For whatever reason, the suffering and pain hikers feel as they move along bubbles to my surface in a very profound manner: great waves of sobbing emerge and tears roll down my unshaven face, triggered by thoughts of home and loved ones. I remember my late father and wonder what he would have thought of his wayward son, worry about my nieces Katie and Lucy, and miss my partner Annie.

The Trail is a constant source of frustration, pain and black despair, but never again does it prompt in me such a powerful expression of emotion and loss. This weeping calms me for the challenges ahead and I don't shed another tear until Mount Katahdin, many months later.

Buoyed up by high emotion, I float along this short section to Hot Springs. At the same time I am more and more part of the land over which I travel and literally never leave it, whether hiking, resting or sleeping.

I know Hot Springs is going to be a good place when I pull up at the Sunnybank Inn, known eponymously as

Elmer's after its owner. Outside is a commemorative marker recording a visit by the English musicologist Cecil Sharp, who documented folk music in the US and UK at the turn of the nineteenth century. It is a good start to a welcome stay in a place of elegance, with a well-stocked library, excellent food and a hammock in which I spend a few days.

In amongst this luxury I spend hours on chores – sealing and gluing my boots which are slowly falling apart, restocking depleted food supplies, moisturising my feet and the painful cracks that have erupted around my toes, repairing clothes and stitching the thermal tops which provided overnight shelter for my adopted family of mice in the Smokies. Concentrating on these tasks takes my mind away from the rigours of the Trail.

I enjoy a hot-spring mineral bath on the banks of French Broad River. Promotional literature from the 1800s claims the facility 'brings vigor to a wasted frame', and I can't put it any better. To get to Damascus in time I have to cover 184 miles in 12 days, or an average of 15 miles per day. I am almost there and my frame is well on the way to being wasted. Resting in water at a temperature of 105°f and drinking chilled Coke while the sun shines and birds sing is miles better than hiking miles.

In Hot Springs hikers quiz me about my Trail name. Thru-hikers have a practice of offering a hiker a name which says something specific about them and which he or she can accept or refuse. Some well-organised hikers come ready prepared with a name, but this can change if an appropriate alternative is offered. Once accepted the name sticks for the rest of the Trail and beyond. Messages pass along the Trail by word of mouth from hiker to hiker and may also be recorded in registers or notebooks found in every shelter. Hikers leave messages using their Trail names; examples include words of encouragement for somebody behind, a reflection on the day or just a name and date. The hiker who leaves the register supplies mailing details on the final page so when it is full another hiker can return it and be rewarded with postage, a photocopy of the complete register and little gift. A hiker's Trail name is important for reasons both practical and symbolic, providing as it does a hugely efficient means of communicating over thousands of miles, without phone or e-mail.

As a result of my lack of preparation I am ignorant of Trail names and I enquire about this rather peculiar practice. One response from Sailman – so named because he lives on a boat – is that it is common practice in hobo communities where people are on the move and persecuted, and anonymity is a good thing. For a bunch of hikers almost to a person middle class and white on a Trail which is as busy as Grand Central Station on occasion, this doesn't quite wash. Another indicates it is to avoid confusing 'real life' names – if there are two Daves, then Trail names differentiate. The fact that I have a very common name has never presented any real difficulty, but the proliferation of Trail names does create a problem – there are two Otters, various Nomads and two Papa Smurfs. The third reason is more acceptable: hikers simply enjoy the romance of adopting a name that says something interesting about them, thus fixing their identity and celebrating one of the Trail's major traditions. It doesn't quite explain the mad rush to anonymity, but the process is clearly enjoyable.

While I'm at Hot Springs hikers busy themselves trying to allocate me a name. Most focus on a national stereotype, suggesting we Scots drink hard, party hard and dislike the English. I am offered 'Wee Drop', my favourite, having expressed great delight with a wee drop of Twig's whisky one afternoon. 'Single Malt' is an offering I take as a measure of class and sophistication on my part (I would have been mortally offended if offered 'Second Rate Blend'). 'Oban', a fine single malt whisky from the West Coast of Scotland, is Diamond Doug's suggestion. The American pronunciation, with emphasis on the b rather than the o, makes it sound like a two-bit town in the South.

I reject 'Beam me up Scotty' because of too many memories of appalling Scottish accents rendered by foreign actors. Likewise anything from Braveheart. 'Kilt Boy' borders on the ridiculous, if only because I haven't worn one since I was ten. I reflect that walking in a lightweight kilt might save problems with chafing, and provide a suitable counterpoint to the small number of male thru-hikers who walk in dresses. The movie Trainspotting has been popular in the US although I'm surprised the language is understood outside Edinburgh, let alone across the Atlantic. After providing reassurance I am not a heroin user and don't live like the characters, we avoid 'Heroin Boy' and 'Begby'.

I remain John, but on occasion I will become Scottish John when hikers leave messages and can't let go of the

Trail name habit.

Here's a taxonomy of Trail names:

Elegant statement of the obvious – Walkin' Home, Pat from Maine, Nomad, Slow but Sure, Wild Child

Play on words – That toe = thattoe = Datto

Profession – Apple works on a fruit farm; Pipeline is an engineer.

Personal interests – Gizmo carries a miniature photographer's studio with him; Data carries an expensive watch and leaves messages in registers with confirmation of time, temperature and altitude.

Physical similarity – Papa Smurf the Senior is a handsome man and much better looking than his name suggests.

Place of residence/personal characteristic – Tex is from Texas; Tuk is a hat from Canada, as is Tuk; Moxie is a root beer from Maine and a description of a forthright personal style – Moxie drinks one and practises the other; Urban Camper derives from a piece of legislation in Atlanta framed to get rough sleepers off the streets.

Statement of coupledom – Yogi & Booboo, B&B, Yak & Yeti

Quote from a conversation – Small World is from the title of the song 'It's A Small World'.

Piece of gear/item of clothing – Split P; Li'l Yellow Bird; Shower Rod – because his mother suggested he bought shower rods rather than hiking poles to save money.

Quote from a Neil Young song – Johnny Rotten spends a week in Las Vegas with Little Princess; Little Princess, in her own words, behaves like one.

Relation to animals – Mousethrower threw a mouse he caught as it ran across his face.

Father and son – Twig & Twiggy

Mother and daughter – Hayride & No Worries

Brothers – Mr Zip carries the advert of the original campaign to launch the zip code and Mr Zap provides back up and moral support.

Dogs and their owners – Winter & Superman, Roanoke & McGruff, Hayden & Amtrak

Sleeping habits – Hacksaw, because he sounds like one; Amtrak, after the US train company, because he snores like a train.

4
Tennessee

North of Hot Springs I meet a keen reader encumbered with various books and a large journal in which he asks me to write a few words. Hikers travel with the strangest items in their packs. Readers and writers impress me most, in part because I manage neither of these activities over most of the Trail. We talk for a while as he tests my interests and capacity for conversation before he retires to his journal.

My sense of history is sharpened in this section because of reminders of both the Civil War and the War of Independence. I rest awhile at the graves of William and David Shelton, Union sympathisers killed by a Confederate force when travelling to a family gathering. There is a third grave, of a young boy. All of them were caught up in somebody else's war.

My capacity for long days of hiking is now established, but I am short of food and go in search of it whenever I can. I try to hitch to a diner on US23 at Sam's Gap with little success – it's a busy road and roadworks make it all the more difficult for cars to stop. I press on within sight of a huge road sign welcoming me to Tennessee and reminding me Al Gore is senator of this proud state.

With Dave, Sailman and Early Bird I lunch on the top of Big Bald, which offers a 360-degree view from over 5,500 feet. It is a stunning spot from which to take in the landscape around us and look back to trace the route we have travelled, although it's never particularly clear. Hiking through a green tunnel has shrunk my sense of direction to the point where there is forward, backwards and very little else. We meet Johnny and Kent out for a day's hiking with Johnny's anxious dog Duck. Johnny is celebrating a recent reprieve from cancer and with a gentlemanly flourish offers a tin of sliced peaches to Early Bird. As a chiropractor approaching the end of her training she knows what is good for her body and eagerly accepts.

We hike with them to Spivey Gap from where they drive us to Erwin as clouds open and rain beats down. The hostel is full and a band is doing a sound check on the porch where everybody, apart from the dogs, is drunk. We move quickly on to Nolichucky campground and check into the bunkroom. The campground is busy with families and large numbers of children swarm around. The place is creaking somewhat and has run out of towels so we shower and dry ourselves with clothes that are dirty and damp. We take time to wash clothes, sort gear and decide what food we require before taking a shuttle into town. The diner is disappointing in the extreme: I have hiked 338 miles for crap food that doesn't quite kill me. Small things plunge me into despair.

Next morning Johnny drives us back to the Gap without our packs, thus allowing us to 'slack-pack'; we float along the twelve miles to the campground, celebrating freedom from the beast on our back before we return to the mountains again.

Some thru-hikers take a resolutely relaxed approach to the process of hiking, choosing instead to drink, smoke and party while moving around by car and hitching. Doing the Trail piecemeal supported by transport of some description is called 'yellow blazing'. For yellow blazers the Trail is a place to sleep, hang out and get close to nature. The attitude of other hikers to these party animals varies from indifference to outright hostility. A few miles above Nolichucky Gorge large numbers of them rest with guitars, drums and miniature tepees. I sit outside my tent listening to their songs and conversations and wondering why I am so focused and they are so relaxed. I will see some of them time and again along the Trail as their schedule takes them from party to party.

After a late night and early start at the Clyde Smith Shelter, from where the journey to the water source is a long hike in itself, Dave and I struggle up Roan Mountain. The mountain has a false peak and I am caught, becoming frustrated and annoyed before I hit the real peak. Struggling up a 4,000-foot gain in three miles is difficult hiking, made even more so by my failure to judge where I am. Hikers travel at two miles an hour on normal terrain, but this slips away to almost nothing when we scramble and haul our way up steep mountain faces. We are on a route of some thirty-four Trail miles when we could hike eight common-sense miles north-east to reach the same spot at

Moreland Gap. But it is worth it for the stunning view, best seen looking south from on top of a pile of boulders, which we race up together, freed from our packs for a few minutes. Birdlife is in abundance and the forthcoming spring continues to make its presence felt.

Near by are the remains of the former Cloudland Hotel, popular in the late 1800s and early 1900s. The Tennessee-North Carolina state line ran through the centre of the hotel's ballroom in order to allow the sale of liquor, legal in one state, but not in the other. There is a foundation stone to remind us of this imaginative use of geographical boundaries to avoid legal ones.

The top is a cold and windy spot where the aggressive Catawba rhododendron now prevails. Dave and I are keen to escape the wind, so after a punishing hike up the mountain we grab lunch. But this is my last peak over 6,000 feet until I reach the White Mountains in New Hampshire and I pause for a cold moment to enjoy the experience. In the mid nineteenth century, botanist Asa Gray called the Roan range 'without a doubt, the most beautiful mountains east of the Rockies', and I can't disagree with him.

Our struggle with Roan Mountain has slowed us and the attractions of Overmountain Shelter some twelve miles after our start prove irresistible. The view is one of the best from any shelter and campsite, strangely reminiscent of Switzerland – high mountains all around, lush fertile valleys, rich green grass, animals grazing in the distance. It has a different look and feel; the first time landscape reminds me of Europe, in part because it is farmed and fertile. The land so far is in its natural state, apart from that blighted by logging. On steep pastures and with a European eye I look for sheep or goats, but it will be months before I realise that with so much land there is no need to make use of every acre.

This shelter is different from the usual three-sided small shed – limited in size, with little if any prospect and dirty. It is a converted barn and I have a prime spot looking out over a valley with nothing to block my view. A Christian group arrive and start singing in a celebration that lasts many hours. A couple call in for water, pulled here and there by an explosion of large dogs in their care. I slip into my sleeping bag early and doze fitfully until offered roasted marsh- mallows, at which point I give up plans for an early night.

One feature of hiking at heights over terrain without cover is that storms can be seen from a distance, often approaching at speed. There is nothing to do apart from take cover or put on waterproof gear. It is an inevitable fact of hiking through three seasons that I will suffer extremes of weather. Next day on top of Little Hump Mountain, which isn't so little at just under 5,500 feet, I see the storm coming. At Bradley Gap I put on waterproofs and the storm hits as I ascend Hump Mountain: cold, biting rain driven by a fierce wind. I prepare to be soaked for the day, but the storm sweeps away into the distance, leaving little behind apart from an over-dressed hiker. The descent of Hump Mountain is swift and uneventful, allowing me time for a second breakfast at the bottom.

Around lunchtime I hear voices up ahead and realise the speakers are in the middle of a full-scale row. I scoot past quickly, acknowledging the couple as I go. Hiking alone is difficult, with new friends it is challenging on occasion, but with loved ones it puts a strain on a relationship beyond anything that has gone before. I eat next to them that night at Moreland Gap Shelter and the argument is now very public. I try neither to listen nor care as I watch another hiker prepare for his evening – Marlboro Reds, freshly percolated coffee made with ground beans and filter papers held by tent pegs, a portable backgammon board and a fetching patterned smoking jacket. I struggle with my stove, running short of fuel and food. My incompetence compares badly with his elegance.

Later that evening Dave and I discuss why, exactly why, we are on the Trail, without coming to a conclusion. It's too early for both of us and we will continue this discussion whenever we see each other. We talk of the traps created by age, career and family expectations and we talk also of our love of the outdoors. Dave works in IT, but like me has a background in social welfare – I suspect the former bores him and the latter has exhausted him. He is doing long miles with a large pack that towers above his slim body. He has a wide taste in music and we quickly discover our shared interests.

Dave's intense blue eyes are framed by dark hair and a beard, but this intensity isn't matched in his conversation, which is soft and gentle in delivery and content – he rarely swears, is unerringly polite and is kind to inexperienced and confused hikers. In moments when I am boiling with frustration or in pain, he unfailingly provides a different, more balanced perspective.

He is one of the few who appear to understand the importance of good eating in the early stages of the Trail and he cooks great meals. Later, when he hears about Robert's tea-drinking habits in Damascus, he will send along a package of dried milk. After Damascus I will never see him again and only catch fleeting glimpses of his name in registers.

The next day I stride away from the shelter and over White Rocks Mountain past a dilapidated fire tower. On the switchback down towards Laurel Falls, there they are, something I have dreaded since starting – a family of bears.

Black bears are not dangerous unless in very specific circumstances; more often they hear hikers and disappear long before they are spotted – and there are no recorded incidents of bears killing hikers on the Trail. I am however terrified because I am unaccustomed to such huge animals in the wild. Most of the family shamble down the mountain into brush and I see a number, two or three including mother, heading away from me. I know I need to keep clear and not get between her and her cubs. It is therefore impossible for me to move on because a cub has scrambled up a tree. It is wedged thirty feet above me in branches, arse pointing skywards towards the heavens, head downhill away from me, stuck there like a pound of lard. I retreat up the hill, mindful of mama. I can't go on, will not go back and my heart is racing fit to burst while my body temperature plummets.

I try clapping my hands together to alert the cub. I blow a whistle attached to my pack within easy reach for this specific purpose. I shout.

No success.

I pick up two small boulders and inch closer before banging them together. The cub turns to look, surprised there is company, before stiffening slightly and shimmying down the tree. He dashes towards mama, thrashing through brush as if the Devil himself is in pursuit. I wait awhile before jogging past, whistle in mouth, boulders in hand, unsure if mama will cuff me for playing rough with junior. As I dash away there is a deep grunt from behind, ensuring I get off the mountain at three miles per hour, twice as fast as normal.

When I reach Hampton, having 'blue blazed' or taken a short cut, I slow down physically and emotionally and recover over a huge breakfast before stocking up at Brown's Grocery, a food and hardware store. I meet an elderly Southern gent who reassures me I did the right thing by keeping away, making as much noise as possible and ensuring the family left before I moved on. He tells me his father once received a cuff when the family dog chased a bear cub and its mother retaliated. We speed through a selection of surnames from his family to identify his European and Scandinavian heritage and I struggle with the challenge of his Southern accent and singsong delivery.

On Watauga Lake I pause for conversation with a hiker weighed down by a huge pack and having ankle problems. He's waiting for his buddies and I'm happy to wait with him, talking myself down over an hour or so. I move swiftly along the lakeside and dam of the same name, watching holidaymakers at play on the opposite banks, before heading towards the ridge. I am jumpy, scanning the woods for signs of movement, ears alert for suspicious noises and constantly wondering what is behind me. It will be a while before I forget my heart-stopping encounter with the bears.

I cook supper as darkness drops at Vandaventer Shelter and am told that a young woman was killed there some years earlier and a whippoorwill bird has visited every night at a certain time ever since. It is not a good start to a long night, which gets worse when a mouse invades my food bag, hanging from the front porch of the shelter, and has to be forcibly removed.

Then the bird arrives. It is named after its call, repeated endlessly and with some volume. I am unsure about my response – to be frightened because of its ghost-like presence; to give thanks for the life of a young woman, brutally foreshortened in this idyllic spot overlooking Watauga Lake; or to lob pebbles at the bird so I can sleep. I lob a pebble and cross my fingers, although the bird returns later to mock me.

On a number of occasions I will stay in or near shelters where hikers have been murdered in previous years. The next time I hear the bird sing is several hundred miles along after a twenty-six-mile hike, which I complete with Urban in eight hours – a significant achievement dampened by discovering the shelter was the site of a double murder. The bird's call is a reminder that all is not necessarily well in this green paradise and rightly features in a Hank Williams song about loneliness and despair. I lie in my tent thinking about what this young couple suffered. Farther along in Pennsylvania there is a shelter that saw a double murder ten years ago and I pause there for a moment in memory of the couple. I cannot and will not go in. The shelter has recently been destroyed and a new one built to commemorate their young lives. I hear talk of hikers armed with pistols, mace, spring-loaded coshes . . . I wonder if these innocent victims would have been better prepared had they had weapons in their packs, but can't believe it would have helped.

Near the town of Damascus is the abandoned farm of a hermit; a memorial to him has been erected by distant members of his family, including a local postmaster now retired. The hermit's memorial reads: 'He lived alone, he suffered alone and he died alone.' I pace up and down, not knowing whether to stay or go, not knowing how to pay my respects to this lonely man. I scribble this quote on the edge of my map and move on, disturbed by what I have seen. In the woods it is easy to lose one's urban veneer very quickly and become a prey to the elements, alone and unprotected.

I will see a number of decaying, abandoned farmsteads along the Trail. At all of them a sense of failure after generations of effort and hard work is pervasive. Land has been cleared, a home built, life engaged with. And then at some time, for reasons only to be guessed at, activity stops. It may be that:

- children go to the city to escape the shackles of farming, encouraged by parents in the knowledge that there is no future in their way of life;
- a family dispute tears the land apart, as brothers and sisters argue over what belongs to whom and how the farm is managed;

- the failing economics of small-scale agriculture mean that the farm can no longer sustain life.

Such places are haunted by memories of those who have worked and died there. In a certain mood, I feel them around me and marvel at how their lives differed from my own. The farms were not just investments or quiet retreats; they were the scene of earnest endeavour over generations.

Their histories are unrecorded so collapsed roofs and drunken fences stand as their testimony, demanding to be read and understood. I never find courage to explore so I gaze from a distance and shudder. I read and understand organisations, but this generational life on the land is beyond me and I have no experience on which to draw, no family history that I know of, and nothing beyond a few novels to guide me. Farming is a vocation, a calling, a familial curse and a hard economic necessity, all of which I avoid. It is difficult to imagine what would persuade me to commit to something so inescapable and demanding, stretching out over time and generations.

That night I spend the evening with Boo Boo, Yogi and a German hiker out for a few days who briefs us about the delights of Damascus.

I moisturise toes and feet that are cracked and bleeding. The pads of my feet look and feel like leather by now, but the soles require lots of Vaseline as well as various creams recommended to me by hikers. The sight of hikers examining each other's ailments while proffering advice, sometimes on the basis of hearsay alone, is always entertaining. I have learned to ignore such homegrown advice, having once been told in South Africa that a poultice of soap and sugar would heal poisoned mosquito bites. My legs still bear the scars of work done by the local doctor after a week of this nonsense. I find myself grateful to my feet and ankles, although it's a strange notion to consider. They are ugly, misshapen things that have caused trouble over the years, usually as a result of too much adventure and exercise. I broke an ankle after falling from the roof of a workmen's hut when I was ten. I have scar tissue from a drunken teenage wander in a paddling pool. No real reason for congratulation here, until I remember they will carry me for over 2,100 miles. Encased in thermal socks and ankle-length leather hiking boots every day for six months, they will force me to stop only once.

My hiking shorts are falling apart, my visible ribs are evidence of a diet ignored, and my boots are splitting again. I stink and my clothes are filthy from sweat and dust. A strong wind whips across the campsite and I lie in my sleeping bag listening to trees swaying and creaking above, hoping there are no dead ones ready to tumble on to this exhausted and lonely hiker.

The next morning I dash into Damascus with Yogi to catch the post office before it closes at 11 a.m. – I have mail waiting for me and am excited at the prospect of hearing from the outside world. Most Americans have food parcels and letters mailed to them on a regular basis, but I rely on the occasional phone call and e-mail. I hear Yogi shout and dash on to discover he has surprised a family of bears. This is my second encounter in forty-eight hours.

On the descent towards town I jog, and this different rhythm makes a pleasant change from striding out, but it does little to stop my bruised feet from throbbing. The Tennessee-Virginia state line is not formally marked so the Mount Rogers National Recreation Area sign sees me do a celebratory jig and whoop with joy as I jump into the air and kick my heels together, while my pack bounces around, out of time with my body.

I am now in the fourth Trail state and it will be another five hundred miles before I exit it; little wonder the 'Virginia Blues', a sense of inordinate effort and no progress, persuades many hikers to go home. By the time I reach Harper's Ferry, West Virginia, some thousand miles along the Trail, fifty per cent of intending thru-hikers will have left.

5
Virginia

Damascus has the reputation of being the friendliest Trail town and it hosts a celebration each May. As I make my way past a wooden pavilion, where preparations are in hand for a yard sale, and over Beaverdam Creek, people greet me, enquiring about my well-being and whether I am enjoying my experience. It is a glorious Saturday in mid-May, the sun shines and people go about their everyday affairs. In my exhaustion, normal life delights and touches me.

I rest at the Apple Tree Inn where Beth and John are watchful as I tend to my bruised and depleted body. I shop for new shorts and socks, eat three times a day, and replace my cooking pot, destroyed in North Carolina when Lewis's bear bag plummeted on to it from fifty feet. At a gas station I receive advice on how to make blueberry pancakes and biscuits with gravy from the owner who is dedicated to good eating.

On Sunday morning I watch as a number of churches fill with worshippers from miles around this small town.

This is the first time I have seen such enthusiasm for and commitment to church attendance. It is part of a broad Southern tradition which accommodates various interpretations of the Bible: some churches allow music and dance, others do not; some welcome speaking in tongues; one holds that true believers are protected from poison and snake bites and so can experience both without fear of death.

In the South they are clear about religion. Clunking poetry on a large poster in a diner near the Smokies reminded me that modern science couldn't explain the workings of the eye or ear and it was best therefore to

Grayson Highlands, Virginia

leave matters to God who, in his wisdom, created everything. Darwinian arguments were dismissed out of hand in this diner, which sold fried food and had huge quantities of cigarettes stacked in cartons around the walls.

On another occasion I hitched a lift in a van emblazoned with various quotations from the Bible to a campsite where the quotations continued on notices around cabins and duck ponds. A hiker, a Vietnam vet and ex-dope-head with a liking for illegal corn liquor, told me straight that his terminally ill brother was in God's hands and my prayers were more appropriate than the thoughts in which I offered to keep him. Along the Trail, I have been meeting hikers who promise to mention somebody or something in their prayers – one even sought guidance on how to keep his tent waterproof.

I stopped attending church when I was ten and have been agnostic and on occasion contemptuous ever since. I expected lots of religion in the US, where even presidents talk about their beliefs and appear to mean it and the majority of the population profess to be believers (although I see little evidence of this in action). I am also aware of the right-wing fundamentalism that attacks abortion clinics and kills in the name of Christ. There are police posters in Trail towns for one of these fanatics and stories of FBI agents posing as hikers in search of the gunman and his supporters.

The passionate intensity of belief, or rather the linear nature of this belief, surprises me. A nation created in part by those fleeing religious persecution displays a marked intolerance towards alien faiths and non-believers. Sometimes people ask me my faith, discover I have none and then move on. Occasionally I sense hostility or a feigned pity. Perhaps I should try harder, but it always feels like a difficult topic – a topic that is almost unbroachable.

The next few days pass in a haze of sleep, food, chores, phone calls and letter writing. I am lucky to receive correspondence from my family with news of life in Cowdenbeath and inspiring notes from nieces busy growing up. Friends send e-mails to keep me in contact with their lives, mocking with details of their last big meal and enquiring about my health. I feel comforted by this interest and walk away from e-mail exchanges with a smile as I think of friends across the world doing their thing.

On Tuesday, 16 May, I wander resplendent in new clothes and waxed boots along Laurel Avenue towards Mount Rogers Outfitters, speeding up as I see my friend Robert in the distance. I ask him if he would prefer to stay in town and enjoy the delights of the forthcoming celebration, but he firmly points me towards the Trail.

I have known Robert for some years, ever since we met while working for a large accountancy firm. He helped me when I was exhausted and fraught with work, guiding me through a number of challenging situations with his wise counsel and support. He calmed me when things were far from calm and inspired me with his commitment and great good humour. Since then we have been friends as our lives and careers have taken us far from the place where we met. I suspect he hopes I will settle down with a good job and wife, but is too polite to give voice to these ambitions. He is a proud father and loving husband so I understand his motivation.

Whenever I travel for periods of time Robert's response is a combination of concern that once again I am taking time off from work and career and an impulse to give me enthusiastic encouragement. In early 2000, when I confirmed my plan to hike the Trail, his wife Jaki immediately called his bluff and suggested he join me: she is the revolutionary in the relationship and he is the reformist. Robert has borrowed, bought and scrounged gear from friends and family. He is honest enough to confess that his exercise regime has not been too demanding, but he is an ideal shape for a hiker – tall with long legs and strong shoulders – and it is this and his well-groomed hair that ensure he always looks great in a tailored suit. He somehow manages to convey the same degree of sophistication in a long-sleeved shirt and cotton trousers with a pack on his back. He does the English gentleman number perfectly and is utterly charming, even when sleeping in a tiny bivouac tent that night and then struggling up Mount Rogers. Robert enjoys the luxuries of life and is accustomed to travelling in comfort and style so he does well to rise to the challenges. The same determination that has made him successful in business also helps him along the Trail.

We head out along a small part of the Virginia Creeper Trail on the route of an old railway line, where I stop to offer whisky to Twig who is cycling with his son. We leave this flat attractive path behind and head up towards

Heading out along an old railway line

the imposing Mount Rogers and on to Grayson Highlands State Park. Robert insists on shaving every morning, producing shaving brush and mirror, embarrassing me with his elegance. He stops regularly for cups of tea to fortify himself for the next stage, a ritual especially necessary when he feels he cannot move another step and one that provides comfort wherever he is in the world.

In the Highlands we hike for days across open terrain and enjoy views uninterrupted by trees. The park is home to wild ponies and we see them scattered around in small family groups; we are careful to ensure our salt-drenched gear is not too readily available – shelter registers are full of stories about gear destroyed by the sharp teeth of ponies after the salt. Robert and I talk and talk, making me realise that although we have known each other over long years, there is still plenty to discover. Surrounded by nature and open to the elements, we plunge into each other's lives.

The Partnership Shelter is an elegant, two-storey construction with air-cooled privy and shower. A telephone is nearby from where orders can be placed with the local pizza restaurant to be delivered by a young man in a car that has seen better days. Robert flourishes his credit card and we eat take-away twice in one day, guzzling pizza and washing it down with litres of soda.

Robert is not an experienced hiker, but hikes with courage and enthusiasm. I am proud of my achievement, but more so of his. We sit in the shelter on his final night and he wishes a gaggle of thru-hikers good luck, suggesting we are all "stark raving bonkers". I think the Americans understand his point. A shuttle collects him the next morning, delivering at the same time a change of clothes, so that he emerges from the restroom his old immaculate self, ready for his trip to NYC and home. His tall body squeezes into the wagon and he pulls away with his arm hanging out of the window, waving as he disappears.

The day he leaves I discover Country Music Television in a motel in Atkins. I ache for music and have enjoyed hitching to town when drivers have radios playing. I naïvely assumed I would hear a variety of live music in small towns, having immersed myself in the Folkways Anthology of American Folk Music before leaving London. Apart from a third-rate cover band in Erwin, Tennessee doing excruciating things to Fleetwood Mac songs and another in Pearisburg, Virginia playing unrecognisable dirges, I will be disappointed. One or two hikers have carried guitars and Tuba Man a thirty-pound tuba on his southbound trip, but I never heard them play.

Scots have a special relationship with country music – we listen to it a lot, concerts sell well and in pub sing-songs when I was a teenager there were a number of favourites offered without fail when people climbed on to tables at the end of a long evening. The melodrama and timeless themes of country music – loss, deprivation, hard men and independent women, the inevitability of life's sufferings – appeal to us. That a number of country music heroes, Johnny Cash in particular, are progressive in their politics may help. We know his concerts at Fulsome Prison and San Quentin are no accident, no mistake made by his agent. Our enjoyment may also be because much country music is maudlin, sentimental rubbish and suits us perfectly. David Thomas playing with the cosmic implications of Stand By Your Man in a piece with the two pale boys is the weirdness of country music made concrete as waves of treated trumpet music wash around.

CMTV displays some of this sentimentality, although performers seem to be turning themselves into rock stars with embarrassing videos, reminiscent of the early days of MTV. Female singers flaunt and male singers pout. The interviews are cringingly embarrassing and I dive under bed covers to hide my blushes. But late at night after a long day's hiking the music is captivating, particularly when old clips are shown, and I will always go a long way for a version of Crazy.

I visit a diner with Urban, BJ and Ham where there is a collecting jar for a local man seriously disabled by terminal illness. Without this paltry change from customers, his chances of getting appropriate medical care are small. I see this poor, wizened man moving around in an electric wheelchair. I will see other collecting jars along the Trail, always in areas where people live from hand to mouth. Never ever in rich areas.

I hike with Urban for the next two weeks. He is a bankruptcy lawyer from Atlanta who has been active in the Trail community. He negotiated time off from his practice and family to hike the Trail, although his wife and children join him at various stages along the way. A few days before we met, he spent time with one of his sons and is clearly missing him. He entertains me with stories of his life, in which he struggles to cope with three young people in the house and parents who sometimes present as many challenges as his children.

His nervous energy drives him on to long miles and days, sustained by little rest and minimal amounts of food; only in towns does he permit himself to eat well. He has an obsessive glint in his eyes and about his face that I recognise when I look in a mirror. He is skin and bone by this time and his clothes and pack seem to hang from his frame. For a man trained in the minutiae of bankruptcy law, he seems to behave in a manner that is far from rational – eating poorly, hiking in sandals, sleeping in shelters and wearing a silk top which is permanently soaked in sweat. I suspect it is his way of celebrating freedom and escape from work and family, by hiking away from those organisational skills that have been with him over his working life.

Urban introduces me to the delights of motels and B&Bs on the Trail and is only half joking when he states he would happily hike from lodging to lodging if the opportunity presented itself.

His short grey hair and beard reinforces an impression of a quiet and thoughtful man, but he is unafraid to puncture arguments which are clearly nonsense with language that wouldn't always be welcome in his smart offices in Atlanta. He is international in perspective and well-travelled compared to many Americans, but he can do the sophisticated-Southern-gentleman number when required and I watch him charm waiting staff in diners and motels with his accent and manners.

After a long hike from Chestnut Knob Shelter, during which time we are buffeted by storms and strong winds, he and I spend an evening with three bikers at a motel in Bland. They think we are crazy for walking so far. We think they are crazy for biking so far and heading off the next day into a storm. Amidst this mutual incomprehension we enjoy an evening, share beers and stories and look out over the Interstate below. The next morning, the bikers are poorly, filling up on nicotine and caffeine as Urban and I move off.

I watch American bikers on their huge machines on long winding roads in glorious weather and at speed. I will fall in love with Harley Davidson motorbikes, particularly after the Blue Ridge Parkway farther north in Virginia, where they move with such grace and sexy elegance. I see a couple, rich baby-boomers with long flowing grey locks, speed past on their 'his and hers' Harleys. The Gold Wings are different beasts – mutton dressed as lamb, motorbikes for ageing men who want some excitement, but not too much.

Urban and I move along at speed and over long distances, but eventually pay a price for our excess. Only on one other occasion along the Trail will my body give up on me, demanding immediate care and attention. On this occasion I hole up in Pearisburg with Urban, both of us nursing swollen, painful ankles with the help of Sam Adams beer, ibuprofen, ice and massage. He is suffering poisoned toes after walking long distances in sandals, so Bearbag lances the affected toes to release the poison and our room looks like a scene from ER with bloodstained towels lying in the corner.

We kill days and pain with countless hours of TV.

C Span is the best of public-service broadcasting and refreshingly earnest for politics junkies. Late one Sunday evening there is an interview with a bloated, raddled

David Crosby who is lucid on American politics and his life and pursues a theme that the sixties did good and harm at the same time. But, how far they have fallen, our heroes who sang with voices like angels.

News channels on TV and cable are truly awful with material repeated every fifteen minutes and little if any detailed investigation of a subject. No debate beyond political posturing, no intellectual engagement, lots of lights. Complex arguments, sometimes involving life and death, are reduced to irrelevance, a lowest common denominator that is below anything I have experienced before. Hikers talk of a small number of well-respected news programmes, but I never find them.

It's all surface stuff which speeds along in a manner that is trance-inducing – a series of sounds and images far removed from reality, allowing us to pass days in a haze of half-memories and distant stimuli. A multiplicity of choice replaces quality, the commercial demands of the media squeezing out good reporting. When I fall into news programmes on occasion I feel the trance deepening; here news is entertainment, and entertainment of this kind is rarely thought provoking.

One cable channel presents the world news in sixty seconds as the presenter speeds through headlines and finishes before time is up. The look of glee on her face is shocking. In the big world out there, where few of you have visited, there is very little happening so don't trouble yourselves with it all now. The Middle East crisis, various emergencies in Africa, the peace process in Northern Ireland are all irrelevant. And have a good night.

The only national channel that appears to be watched and discussed by all is the twenty-four-hour Weather Channel. 'Yup, it will be sixty degrees today with a fifty per cent chance of rain.' This is stone-dead weirdness at its best – forget hallucinogenic drugs, stop drinking corn liquor and lay off grass. Burn your copies of American Psycho, Fear and Loathing in Las Vegas and On the Road. Watch the Weather Channel instead. It employs ranks of presenters who get very excited about weather for long periods of time, while being unerringly polite to each other. Editors use all sorts of techniques to keep their presenters fresh and vibrant in the pursuit of excellence. Amidst the swirling, speedy computer graphics and the chemically fuelled excitement of the presenters, I really want them to say, 'John Scott, today on the Trail the weather will be delightful and you will suffer not one jot. The weather is with you and your friends. Go well.' They never do.

Late one Sunday evening Urban and I watch Prime Minister's Question Time from London, and I conclude I'm not really all that daft to be on the Trail. I wonder why some senior US politicians are so keen to copy the format until I realise they see its huge entertainment potential. The process is nothing to do with democracy or parliamentary accountability, it is entertainment. Gil Scott Heron knows it is only revolutions that are not televised. As the UK parliamentarians josh about Tony Blair's newborn son, I am embarrassed to be represented by this bunch of buffoons.

The motel's owner tells her son as he heads out for the evening that she don't want no Oreo cookies around the house. It takes me a while to realise she is worried about her son having a child, black on the outside and white on the inside, with a black girlfriend. Later I will hear another motel owner comment that competition from Asians is unfair because they rely on their families for free labour. Such casual racism is blatant and unforgiving. I will encounter it infrequently.

Urban and I slowly venture out of town, both of us amazed our legs, feet and toes are functioning, allowing us to push hard towards McAfee Knob, rightly famous for the manner in which it cantilevers out and suspends hikers in thin air. For me it is the changing landscape below that catches my attention, and I see large swathes of farmland, cultivated areas and clusters of towns for the first time. After 700 miles we emerge from the rural south, heading towards the industrialised north. This spot marks my progress, my long journey through America. Descending from McAfee to hike for a further fifteen miles, Urban and I feel the absolute power of summer hit us with a temperature of 90°. We carry little water and lose a water bottle so arrive in Roanoke exhausted, dehydrated and burnt.

My happiest experiences on the Trail have been a combination of hard, difficult hiking and stunning views where there isn't much else to see apart from more mountains. Such space and wilderness are things to be celebrated. Hiking in the Virginian lowlands is exciting for different reasons as I enjoy sneaking through large populations of real people, making the most of access to proper food and proximity to various cities. But the excitement of months ahead in the lowlands will not really compare with time in the mountains.

Trail Angels appear in the strangest of places. North of Roanoke after a long wet day which leaves me soaked and exhausted I am relieved as rain slows, mist drops and a couple arrive at the Punchbowl Shelter with home-baked bread, apple butter, fresh fruit and vegetables. The Angels take photographs with the promise they'll be at the celebration in Damascus in 2001 if I want to see my dirty, smiling mug on show.

Farther along one of our company dies from a heart ailment. I camped with him at the base of Cold Mountain on a glorious spot and he taught me how to make better use of my camp stove. I have thought of him most nights when putting my stove together. The news of his death travels quickly through the Trail community and shocks us in different ways. We are celebrating life's potential and diversity so it is a cruel blow when one of us is taken in the midst of such blessing.

At Punchbowl I camp next to a pond with a bullfrog population. I haven't been aware of bullfrogs until now, apart from ads for a rather insipid US beer. As darkness descends, the bullfrogs get louder and more persistent until in the early hours of the morning there is a full-scale orchestra tuning up. The double-bass, percussion and tuba sections are well represented, the sonic effect of the pond is suggestive of large echo chambers and the orchestra's grasp of crescendo is impressive. The musicians benefit from significant stamina and the concert lasts until dawn.

I emerge at Rockfish Gap to spend a few days in Waynesboro in preparation for the Shenandoah National Park. Americans talk of the Lewis and Clark expedition, which opened up the West Coast in the early nineteenth century, as though it was yesterday, and are proud of their achievements. Lewis grew up near the Gap. Books about the expedition sell well and websites abound with debate and discussion. Few however talk of Lewis's struggle with his devils and eventual suicide. Few reflect on the destruction unleashed on American Indians as a consequence.

There are parts of the Trail that demand celebration solely because they exist. The Shenandoah National Park is one such – breathtaking landscape with excellent facilities. It is rich in wild life and plants and protected by friendly rangers. When darkness falls and cars reduce to a trickle, animals come out to reoccupy road and verge, reminding us it is their home and we are only passing through. A number of hikers take time out to 'aqua blaze' by canoe through the park in an imaginative counterpoint to the boredom of hiking every day.

Deer, Shenandoah National Park

In Glasgow, Virginia, a man told me I could expect to see bears on a daily basis in the Shenandoahs and reassured me I might be wet, but would never freeze now that summer was upon us. Animal mores are strictly non-PC, so there are no reconstructed egos in male bears or deer, no new men in the woods, no Iron John sessions round the water source. Males have their way, occasionally seeing off a rival and then leave the mother to look after the offspring. So this large bear shuffling towards me is definitely male. I saw another bear in a hollow on the second day in the Shenandoahs. He looked at me a while, shrugged his shoulders with languor and ambled off. This one is a different challenge in that he's bigger, travelling at quite a pace and has yet to see or hear me. I remember I shouldn't catch a bear's eye, which is difficult advice to follow because I sure as shit don't want to look away while he approaches. I clap my hands three times and he disappears off to my left. I remain strangely calm throughout and never see a bear again.

Rain brings out salamanders that are hugely vibrant in colour to frighten predators. I skip lightly past them as they freeze, having sensed my thundering approach; their legs shift together in a mechanistic pre-programmed fashion, guided by pneumatic pumps in their tiny bodies. In a world of green and brown and stone, they are an entertaining diversion.

I see large turtles with multi-coloured shells in the strangest places – hundreds or thousands of feet up a hill, miles from water and casually taking in the day as they move along. They watch the world with heads extended from their shells and hovering in the air, supported by impossibly thin and wrinkled necks. The shell patterns are varied and fascinating, coated with layers of what could be heavy-duty yacht varnish. In their imperturbable silence and regal bearing they remind us of their ancient heritage. They appear from nowhere and return from where they came.

On my final morning in the park I am booked for sleeping in the wrong place, a delightful picnic spot I found after a long day's hiking just as darkness fell. I have a photo of Small World and me taken as the sun set; we are on fire, surrounded by bushes blazing in the night. The site seemed too good to be true, but a park ranger thinks differently the next morning. He takes my passport as identification and tells me I'll get a penalty point that will remain for three years. When he is taking my details I get too close to him and he gestures me away. I realise he is heavily armed and wearing body armour under his shirt. He deals with poachers who are much less supportive of his activities than a sleepy, hungry thru-hiker, but he responds warmly to my words of apology and embarrassment.

At the exit from the park heading north towards Front Royal the landscape changes to broken rock, stunted bushes and bare earth, as if the land has run out of energy necessary to sustain this beauty and needs to pause for breath.

6
West Virginia

On 4 July in celebration of Independence Day and my exit from Virginia I enjoy a good lunch at the 'psychological' thousand-mile halfway point of Harper's Ferry, West Virginia. The town partied a few days before and the streets feel like my hometown on 1 January: everybody is tucked up in bed recovering, trying to find a comfortable place for poisoned body and aching mind. I plan to hike on, but lunch, heat and exhaustion convince me to stay over.

There have been and will be many spots along the Trail where I celebrate a statistic – the first week, 500 miles with Robert, the next 200 with Urban, right now the 1,000-mile point in good weather, the 2,000-mile mark will be painted in yellow and marked by flaccid balloons on a forest road in Maine, and each of the boundaries between fourteen states.

These celebratory points mark my progress through America. I remembered every mile of the first five hundred, but thereafter my memory falters and I find myself checking maps and reference books to confirm I did indeed cover such and such a distance. They all add up on paper, but not quite in my mind because the numbers are too big and achievement already great. My niece captures the predicament when she points out I will walk nearly three return railway journeys from Edinburgh to London.

As I flip through the Data Book during my ritual of checking progress and miles, images jump to mind and I want to record them before they slip away over time. The individual images are stunning and their totality is overwhelming, summing up as it does my entire Trail experience so far. When I read in this frame of mind I manage only a handful of pages before I must stop, so rich are the stimuli. But hardly a day goes past when I don't return to it, dipping in like a wee boy raiding a biscuit box. Never before has my life been so eventful and picturesque, full of pictures and images. It is a technicolour experience, which constantly triggers memories and associations. It is a way of seeing my life through nature and my fascination with this country.

Each statistic fills me with joy, sometimes fuelled by whisky, allowing me to move on to the next milestone. I learn not to count each day and worry away at my cumulative total because that path is marked 'frustration and disappointment'. After three months and this many miles, I know that the rest will rush past and my return flight will soon be upon me.

One key element of my joy is the Trail itself. Hiking along on any old day in Trail-time, it is easy to forget what a huge achievement this represents for the American people and those charged with protecting this treasure.

Hikers take it for granted and are woefully ignorant, on occasion, of the mechanics of its upkeep. The Trail is the result of young men's dreams, a fairy-tale come true. In these cynical, post-modern times I take comfort from an achievement that has delivered so much. In its place could be barbed-wire fences, ski resorts, private housing estates and large farms. In short, it could look like the rest of the country. Instead it offers a welcome to people who wish to escape to the wilds and experience nature.

A small number of individuals pushed this project forward over time, with great foresight and imagination. These are not skills normally associated with public servants or planners. In the conception and delivery of a 2,100-mile footpath through fourteen states, their vision was revolutionary, nothing more and nothing less. The Grandes Randonnées or GR in France are long and impressive, but lack a similar level of public support, infrastructure and imagination. It is almost impossible to conceive what a twenty-first-century equivalent might look like in any other country across the world.

The time it took to build the path was significant, given the difficulty of the terrain, although much of it in early years was along forest and public roads. This should not demean the efforts involved, which were and remain considerable. It was completed in a relatively short time within a limited budget and I am reminded of this when I see large public projects run over budget, like the Big Dig in Boston or the Millennium Dome in London. Sizeable public projects rarely run to budget or fulfil original expectations, and the extra costs and disappointments are borne by the public, never planners or politicians. Large private projects sometimes suffer the same fate, although in their case costs are fed back to the consumer or shareholder. Some of Mitterand's Grand Projets are an exception and now grace Paris as elegant monuments to the power of public spending and civic imagination. Other examples are rare.

The Trail also surmounted significant legal and technical difficulties in relation to land acquisition and leasing, evidence that private interest and official apathy can be overcome.

It is the best of things American – imaginative and bold, an exciting celebration of the wilderness but accessible to all, federal in structure and participative in approach, publicly owned, a little miracle. I have travelled all this way in miles and years to celebrate my confused relationship with the US, prompted almost entirely by cultural and political interests, only to discover it is the land which captures me and points me towards a clearer understanding. In modern America it would be impossible to develop the Trail from scratch, so much have things changed. The barriers are now too big. This should encourage us to celebrate the Trail's existence all the more.

The organisation responsible for managing this national treasure is based in Harper's Ferry. I expect to find the Appalachian Trail Conference closed on this very special public holiday and so to miss the traditional opportunity of having my photo taken and filed in a binder, along with those of other smelly thru-hikers. To my surprise there is a volunteer on duty with coffee, fruit muffins and jokes about independence from us Brits. Sure, have it all.

The binders indicate how much has changed over the twenty-five years since the collection began. In the seventies there were fewer women hikers and men wore long hair and untrimmed beards as an overt rejection of consumerism, not shaving and leaving their hair to grow for the entirety of their hike. Now there are more women and clean-cut hikers are not unusual.

The ATC is a joy to deal with. Its staff and volunteers respond swiftly to requests for information. The quality of documentation and advice is excellent. Telephone calls and e-mails are returned promptly. Concerns are addressed without delay. Begging letters for extra funds are few and existing funds are managed with care. There is a marked desire to consult with members and volunteers. If only my bank was so efficient. If only the other charities I support were so considerate. This efficiency was not my experience alone but also that of other users over a period of some twelve months. Andrew, Robert and Annie all benefited from the ATC's advice and publications when planning trips to join me.

One reason for the ATC's success is its dependence on a network of volunteers and a federal structure of autonomous clubs stretching along the Trail. It avoids the arrogance of a large organisation and has to be permanently sensitive to its members, however they are defined. I'm sure the clubs are mindful of their status and keen to protect both geographical and organisational boundaries. The clubs vary in structure from hand-to-mouth operations to big-money facilities with full-time staff. This diversity of approach and devolution of decision-making within a federal structure is not something I have experienced. The mechanics must be time consuming and frustrating on occasion, and I can't quite see how decisions are made quickly. Everybody has a view on everything, which they feel they have the right to express fully, irrespective of whether anybody is interested. Debates rage in journals, via websites and on the Trail about whether shelters are a good idea, how best to cope with increasing levels of human use and the legitimacy of travelling without a pack by slack-packing. But it all works splendidly.

Another reason for its success is the strong sense of history and tradition that permeates the organisation and Trail community. When disputes arise, participants often turn to its purpose and role for resolution, constantly using this 'external good' as a point of reference. In this way there is an emphasis on free and open access, thrift and careful investment and a strong sense of managing a resource for the use of future generations. A number of heritage and outdoor organisations in the UK adopt a similar approach, admittedly not always with the same commitment to access, but somehow this leads to an organisational conservatism, possibly because the role of volunteers in the organisation is in helping rather than managing the organisation.

I don't have a sense of this conservatism with the ATC, although some of its more radical environmentalist members might disagree. I suspect it has a keen sense of strategy which allows adaptation to change: the first phase opened the Trail, the second protected permanently the path and its surroundings by acquisition, the third and current phase is making its resources better known. This phase chimes neatly with a growing focus on outdoor education and increasing awareness of the nation's natural heritage. This focus is timely as the Trail and its minders struggle with the problem of over-use in some areas. It is both public profile and level of use by all sections of the community that will ensure further success. For observers of organisational strategy, this is classic stuff and provides a sense of constant renewal and struggle, fuelled by energy and success.

While I am in Harper's Ferry a thru-hiker asks if as a Brit I object to the Independence Day celebrations. The question leaves me shocked. What is it to do with me? Are my views on self-determination for independent countries likely to be so shabby? But, of course, the question is a sincere one – in a country with a strong sense of its own history, it is easy to assume we Brits are still bitter at the recent loss of what was ours. And yet it is difficult to imagine even the most right-wing of English patriots worrying too much at the loss of colonies at a time when they are busy fulminating against Europe. In the debate about the future of Zimbabwe as it careers towards economic collapse and political authoritarianism, there is little braying about the benefits of white rule.

This experience confirms in my mind that America likes its traditions, even when they are not all that old. In a country where the Civil War is still being enacted and argued over, what matters the passing of years when sacred principles are at stake? When the national flag and various state flags are sources of pride and fierce dispute, what matters historical fact?

I engage in more conversations about my ancestors, even the most recent of whom I know very little, than at any other stage in my life so far. My accent is enough to send large numbers of Americans into stories about their family origins, describing assortments of European and Scandinavian ancestors all making their way to God's own country to escape religious or political persecution or just to find a better life. Clear memories of events sometimes centuries old, supported by family stories and an active interest in genealogy, pour out, along with minute calculations of the percentage of German, Scottish or Swedish blood in them.

I am embarrassed that I barely know what my great-grandparents did and certainly have little idea of the history of my clan. I was however happy to confess twice on the same day in Virginia that I did not know if I was related to the kings of Scotland, unlike my questioners who both claimed direct descent. Clans are a relatively recent invention and their histories suffer from flights of imagination rather than historical fact. It is not clear whether clans acted in any unified manner against the enemy, English or French, but I was unsure if a debate on the subject was in order. We were in the land of myth and magic rather than known facts so I said little and avoided denting the myth.

This fascination with the past may, on occasion, be camouflage for racism, religious intolerance and bigotry. Historical events are rarely well documented, the intentions of those involved entirely unambiguous and the consequences unequivocally in favour of one side or the other. In truth, much of what passes for popular history is an exercise in imagination and wishful thinking.

And yet I think I now better understand why Americans flock to Europe in search of family connections: in a rootless, young society which comprises so many nationalities, usually torn from 'home', living in a huge and hugely populated nation, the search for historical certainty and sense of belonging must be powerful. In a nation where large numbers of people appear to be permanently on the move, the desire for stability is deeply felt. The fact that much of this historical certainty is newly constructed and doesn't withstand critical review is irrelevant. What is relevant is that people 'feel' their history and it is important to them, providing an identity and location over centuries and thousands of miles. We Europeans can afford to be contemptuous of such matters, cushioned as we are by the luxury of long history.

Walking out of Harper's Ferry, one finds history underfoot – an old canal, one of a few along the Trail, starting from Washington DC and stretching for over eighty miles. I enjoy the C&O canal because it's flat and runs along the elegant Potomac River. Now used as a cycling route, it is a perfect green artery from the heart of a heartless city, a city disfigured by the presence of too many politicians and public servants, a place where uniforms abound.

Most canals near the Trail are failed experiments in water transportation, built by entrepreneurs beaten by the arrival of the railways. Some failed because of penny pinching on the part of builders and one constantly leaked water from the beginning and was never cured. Others failed because of intransigent behaviour on the part of owners. The movement to protect this industrial heritage for leisure use and outdoor education is making progress.

The canals seem over-ambitious in their aims and slightly ridiculous in such a huge country. The regret I feel is not the manner of their failure, but rather that their successors are woefully inadequate. The modern passenger-train network is slow, incomplete, expensive and loathed by all. In over 2,100 miles through some of the most densely populated parts of the nation, I was rarely within striking distance of a passenger train. Only recently has a high-speed connection between NYC and Boston opened, and even that is expensive and not really high-speed – merely faster than its very slow predecessor.

Advice in Trail manuals reminds hikers to check train times because of frequent changes and not to rely too much on published arrival times. I think of France and Switzerland with their state-subsidised and hugely efficient train services, and of long journeys between these two countries conducted in style and comfort. Indeed the services of some supposed third-world countries are better. If neo-liberalism as applied to public policy means anything to the people of the US and UK, it means crap public transport.

But freight trains are different.

Freight trains are stunning, snaking along for miles with cargoes of car parts, logs and coal; the long, echoing whistle wakes me in the night and it haunts me. Here is a technology that is functional and magical and deserves to be celebrated. If any sound captures my time on the Trail, it is the whistle of a freight train, reminding me of Casey Jones, a widely forgotten TV programme from the black-and-white era which my sister and I watched while we waited for our father to return from work. I only just remember Mr Jones, but I can clearly hear the whistle.

7
Maryland & Pennsylvania

Maryland is a short Trail experience stretching forty miles from the Potomac River to Pen Mar Park. This presents the next hiking challenge for those who want to hike a long distance in a twenty-four-hour period, which at an average speed of two miles per hour over easy terrain is not impossible. I am averaging fifteen to twenty miles per day and now take advantage of relatively easy hiking conditions, but am unwilling to push my body to a point where I do more damage.

Instead I head to Washington DC for a few days of rest and relaxation. I worship at the White House, remembering how decisions taken in this place and taught in school influenced my teenage years. I eat, sleep and eat again. And I spend ninety dollars on an emergency filling for a tooth that has been troubling me for weeks. Having covered over a thousand miles I am happy, but I know there are still eleven hundred left and both terrain and weather will turn against me in the months ahead. This is the first city I have visited since Atlanta in mid-April and I am keenly aware of the nearby airport, my route home to comfort and relaxation.

Returning to the Trail I find a note from Urban confirming he was in the area a week earlier and took time off to see his family. I am chasing him and a number of other hikers, keen to meet up, but knowing the chances of doing so are slim because a week is a long time when measured in miles.

I meet members of a black evangelical church, weighed down by tons of camping gear, including a huge oil lamp, but buoyed by their relationship with God, cheerful and joyous at the same time. They stagger along talking and singing, disarmingly unprepared for their experience. As they go they marvel at the beauty of God's creation, gazing around the forest in wide-eyed appreciation. They think we are crazy for hiking such a long way. 'Have a good evening, sleep well and may God go with y'all.' They need the gear for a night at the Pogo Memorial Campsite – I'm unsure who Pogo was, but he enjoyed sleeping on rocks.

I think back to school lessons on the Civil Rights movement and know there is now a sizeable black middle-class population in the US. In my hiking experiences across the world, one thing was self-evident: hiking was an activity for middle-class whites. Perhaps, I thought, the Trail was going to be different and blacks will have moved into a space once populated by whites, but I am wrong again – in six months hiking, I saw only this church group (obviously at odds with its surroundings), two black and two Asian hikers.

I have hiked though rural populations before and there has always been some puzzlement on the part of local people as to why I hiked. It was not a walk to market to sell or buy goods so it had no economic benefit, although I brought hard currency with me as a tourist; it was not a ritual or religious activity, or at least I didn't believe it to be such; I was not going to a family celebration, although I was celebrating; it was for my pleasure and a perverse pleasure it appeared to be; I was walking long distances for no good productive reason whatsoever in terms of my material or religious well-being; I was not doing penance or buying credit with my maker in advance of meeting with him, or at least it didn't feel like it; and I was equipped with specialist gear which represented great wealth wasted on a luxury of limited use rather than invested in immediate survival. I have never found a satisfactory way of explaining my love of hiking to local people who are tied to the land.

A young black man in South Africa once remarked to me that hiking was for whities and walking long distances was for the ancestors. In this neat summary he made clear his distaste for outdoor activities – he wanted a car to relieve him of the effort of moving around on foot and to ensure his leisure time never focused upon the outdoors. Black communities move away from land that imprisoned them, while whites return to places once colonised by them for the purpose of outdoor activity.

Now not only am I walking with whites, I am moving through white communities; apart from in Atlanta, Georgia and Peekskill, NY, I see very few people of colour in Trail towns. There are Indian and Bangladeshi families running motels, but not too many as yet.

It is strange that in some of the most densely populated parts of the nation, the vast majority of the population is white. It leaves a sense of something missing from my experience of the Trail and while I read of the growing numbers of Latinos, the influx of professionals from Asia and the successes of the middle-class black community, it all remains hearsay. When I raise this issue on the Trail, people just shrug their shoulders as if it's not a puzzle to them or not something they consider.

In a restaurant farther back in Virginia a black family had arrived and been ushered into another room. Urban looked awkward and felt the need to apologise because they were being fed in separate facilities and he was ashamed. I assumed they were smokers, were in the smoking room, and fortunately I was right. But Urban is in his fifties and has seen such behaviour before in his short life, in the last half of the twentieth-century. Perhaps the circle is not yet complete and is still full of gaps. My studies of the Civil Rights movement concluded over twenty years ago, and yet I am left with an impression that not a lot has changed.

Schoolboy memories continue as I hike close to Camp David on my way to Pen Mar Park and struggle to remember lessons about agreements struck here. On a Sunday in July, I emerge into the park and am greeted by the sight of great swathes of seniors dancing under a bandstand as others eat hot dogs and drink soda. It is a surreal experience to be among these good people celebrating long years with the two-step and waltz, providing such a vivid display of vigour and good health. A number of seniors comment they can't hike because it is too difficult, but I watch them swirl over the dance floor with skill and precision and I wonder. My legs now lock whenever I stop for any period of time, I stagger as muscles loosen when I move off and my body is unused to any movement apart from hiking. So my capacity to dance is indeed limited, but I've met many seniors along the Trail, so I know that they can hike.

I go to the café on a number of occasions and gaze with wonderment and open-mouthed surprise at normal life happening around me. In the restrooms I delight in flushing toilets and running water. I converse on matters as varied as the weather, the Trail and Scottish history. I discover that the nearby railway line used to bring thousands of city dwellers to the countryside to enjoy the fresh air and landscape. A freight train pulls past and its whistle gives thanks to those who have gone before. I feel a part of living history.

All the time I am made welcome as senior after senior approaches with questions, advice and requests for photos. They move off slowly at the end of day, waving goodbye and wishing me well, packing cars and pick-up trucks with belongings, and the sprawling car park empties. The Data Book now provides ample evidence of the effect of cars upon the US countryside as the Trail moves through areas of high-density population and across major roads and interstates with increasing regularity. Now I often fall asleep to the sound of traffic rather than the sounds of nature.

Americans love cars with a passion, but their love affair with the car has its basis in economics. There is literally no other choice. Those who use Greyhound or other coach services do so because they can't afford cars or planes. And they do so at some risk. The drivers are fine, but the passengers are often crazy and volatile. On one occasion when I travel by coach, a driver hears my accent and suggests I sit up front. I have never seen so many people talking to themselves as I have on a Greyhound coach. Later when I finish the Trail I travel to Boston from Maine by a coach on which a lady is loud and persistent in her explanation of various conspiracy theories. Those at the bottom of the heap, who can't afford coaches, hitchhike and are usually ignored, written off by drivers as insane.

It is the logic of the market at its extreme – a hierarchy of provision governed by money, a hierarchy of need subverted by commerce. It is also a market stamped by prejudice – the few times I see blacks and Latinos is when I travel by Greyhound: there they make up the majority of the passengers.

In a nation where the car is worshipped and deified, I now understand why it makes great good sense to collect five or six and leave them rusting in the front yard.

In a café before Pine Grove Furnace State Park a number of hikers gather to eat ice cream and celebrate the almost-halfway-mark up ahead. There is a Trail practice of eating a gallon of ice cream, in return for which the café provides a prize of a small wooden spoon. Bernie adds to his achievements of these past few months by carefully tucking away a gallon, while others fail with some aplomb.

It is now summer and so I see lots of kids on the Trail, encouraged by parents to experience the great

The ice cream challenge

wilderness because, in some perverse sense, it is good for them. There is a word in Cowdenbeath for this feeling of being sick to one's soul – the kids are 'scunnered'. I pass a Jewish youth club out for a trek, with some of the most miserable looking kids dragging themselves along. One little girl is at the back, shoulders dropping, feet barely moving, eyes boring into the ground. Some months later I will meet Matt who runs an outdoor centre in Maine. He tells of college kids who go into the woods as part of their induction programmes and some find it so shocking they can neither pee nor poop, so frightened are they. They start their college years with a terrifying experience and constipation.

I see two young Mennonite ladies in floral-patterned skirts and hats dozing on the side of the Trail and disturb their holy rest when I pause for a voyeuristic moment.

They wake, smile at my disbelief and wish me well. I conclude they look out of place before realising I myself hardly blend into the woods.

I only ever meet one kid who is full of the joys of outdoor life, a rather overweight Boy Scout in Boiling Springs. He is joyous and proud of his five days and four nights on the Trail and it marks him in a way that will last for ever. He chats to me about this experience while his friends mope around, dreaming of showers and pizza. Over the next few days I discover a number of hikers who have been lifted by his enthusiasm. This young boy doesn't realise he cheers us all by his example.

Pennsylvania displays its industrial heritage like no other state on the Trail – The Deer Hunter was filmed here because of its combination of heavy industry (now no more) and wilderness. The character played by Christopher Walken talks with embarrassment of his love for trees and suggests it is this that takes him out of the steel town and not a desire to hunt. I can't explain my love of trees any better.

Bethlehem is no longer a steel town and there is now an abundance of smart coffee shops along Main Street. I studied the development of US and UK steel industries in geography class at school so know of the almost mythical status of Bethlehem. The myth is dead and steel men are nowhere to be seen, leaving behind the smart houses which once belonged to owners and managers and a polluted site.

I wander along the Trail and begin to find that the paths sprinkled with coal dust and 'bings', large mounds of coal workings covered by plants on both sides, look strangely familiar. In Pennsylvania evidence of coal extraction remains although the communities that comprised large numbers of mining families are gone. These communities saw strikes, attempts to unionise, pit disasters, the effects of coal miner's lung, the encroachment of cheap foreign coal and competition from other energy sources. I grew up in a coal-mining community so I recognise all the signs.

Duncannon is a working-class town which has seen better days and there the Doyle Hotel is a legendary favourite for hikers, although the standard of accommodation has never been high. A hiking couple, James and Veronica, stun the barmaid by refusing a room – the first time it has happened, she tells them – and take their business elsewhere, having promised themselves not to compromise too much on life's necessities. As soon as I see rooms at ten dollars a night I know the territory.

They are generous people in Duncannon. I wander along Main Street past employees from UPS on a recruitment drive – if I give them my address and fill in an application form, I'll get a free ice cream. I confess I'm not their best catch for various reasons, but I get a free ice cream anyway. I'm told to order a small one and then discover why when a multi-storey concoction, which the cone can barely support, is passed to me. It's good quality and rests nicely on top of a huge lunch from a nearby diner and various snacks.

In the first shelter after town hikers reflect on their Doyle experience – erecting tents inside the rooms to protect themselves from the squalor, wondering why the local Hygiene Department is so hopeless, hanging food bags to protect food from mice, feeling like an extra from a Tarantino movie, thinking of the shooting galleries in Trainspotting.

We hoot with laughter and hope not to bump into the young bear that has been following hikers; he has been thrown out of the family group at a certain age and is having difficulty making his way. Being fed by hikers is encouraging him to approach more aggressively, and if he gets too troublesome he will be moved by rangers. If this fails, he will be shot.

Andrew is joining me from England to hike in Pennsylvania and New Jersey for a week. Leaving Mr Fine's Fine Board & Lodgings in Slatington, I walk along the street to see Andrew's long legs stretching across the sidewalk, pack neatly beside him as he rests his skinny butt on the ground.

Climbing a steep, rocky hill in blazing sun out of town, we see the impact of thirty years of zinc processing. The land is poisoned, rocks symbolically misshapen and water supply suspect. I choose to go thirsty rather than run a risk. I suspect local people rue the closure of the plants, imposed by the Environmental Protection Agency; in return for degradation of their environment, they received well-paid work, as had their parents before them. They bought houses, large cars, invested in the future, and encouraged their children to follow them and enjoy the same relatively high levels of income.

Andrew and I have known each other for many years, but this is the first time we have done any outdoor activity together. I assume because he is a marathon runner he will be fine with the distance to be covered and discomfort involved. He soon puts me right – the advantage of running is that it's done in a few hours, after which a hot shower and good food are to hand. We walk through some of the rockiest terrain on the Trail, his pack too heavy until we get to a post office to mail items home, and his boots fall apart. The discomfort gets to him although he does well in the circumstances, in part by finding as many motels and hostels as possible and even a Chinese massage at Delaware Water Gap.

Hikers are easy prey to extremes of temperature, severe weather, hunger, thirst and ill health. My friends and family suspect as much and find ways to steer clear. My mother agrees to join me if she can have a nap every day, bring her car and knitting. I accept her conditions, but she never arrives. Dave will join me from Edinburgh as long as he doesn't have to walk. Sue will join me from Hong Kong via New York if the hotels are good.

There is a very real threat to health. Within a day or two of Slatington a nasty bite on Gizmo's thigh is causing concern. It is ugly, swollen and weeping pus and may mean that he has Lyme disease, which brings with it the possibility of meningitis, encephalitis and arthritis and recurring bouts of pain and discomfort. Daily checks for ticks, particularly deer ticks that carry Lyme, become boring after a few days of the routine in summer and it is difficult to distinguish between hiking debris – mud, leaves, small pieces of grit – and ticks, but the disease is unpleasant in the extreme. Along the Trail I will meet Dog and discover he had a month in hospital as a result of a new vaccination for Lyme or a bite. He walks with treated dog collars on each knee in an attempt to avoid the curse. I redouble my efforts to find the tiny beasts before they burrow into my skin and leave their poison behind.

Gizmo's wound might also be the bite of the Brown Reclusive spider; necrotic in effect, it leaves behind gaping wounds and the need for reconstructive surgery. It is a spider bite that will persuade Papa Doc to leave the Trail in New York, having been told by his doctor he needs treatment or risks losing his foot.

Before treatment commences Gizmo has to convince his insurance company he can be treated outside the geographical area covered by his policy. Fortunately the manager at the insurance company is a hiker and therefore sympathetic otherwise the cost will run into thousands of dollars and Gizmo will have to meet this from his own limited funds. And neither Lyme disease nor the Brown Reclusive waits for cash or credit.

There are other fixed sources of discomfort. I am always wet with sweat while hiking and by the end of the day clothes are soaked. Hiking clothes are almost impossible to dry overnight: I rescue shorts and T-shirt from the bottom of my tent each morning and pull them on, damp and smelly. Hiking socks last for three to four days before feeling as though they might crack if bent too far. My mother is shocked when she discovers after several months that I shower every five or six days and am only carrying two T-shirts. I think she's ashamed she brought up an untidy midden rather than proud he has found the perfect means of existing several thousand miles away. In the summer months from Virginia until New Hampshire I suffer from chafing and walk with a pot of

Vaseline in my pocket. I apply it around my groin, up my bum and around my waist, and hope there are no photos of me with hand down my shorts and a look of concentration on my face.

I now know why babies cry so when they have nappy rash – it is painful and is made more agonising by the slightest movement. Damn right they should cry, and I nearly do on a number of occasions. Hikers go a long way for containers of Gold Bond talcum powder, a magic antidote. Some are surrounded by clouds of the stuff when they move off in the morning.

There is also an absolute lack of comfort to be relied upon from sleeping bag and mat – I am over six foot and like to stretch out when sleeping. My bag trusses me and wakes me when arms and legs become trapped. I never remember my dreams, but I'm sure they are about huge comfortable beds in temperature-controlled silent rooms with en-suite facilities, including unlimited amounts of hot running water. And a well-stocked fridge.

8
New Jersey & New York

Leaving Delaware Water Gap is difficult because the weather is poor and Lynda, Andrew and I are tired, having crossed the 'Pennsylvania Rocks', infamous for rock and rubble along the path and talked of since Springer. The rocks are not as bad as Trail myth suggests, but are still difficult and damage unprotected feet and legs. A couple from New Zealand are having difficulty – she is in pain with ankles that swell and bloat, he is exhausted with efforts to keep them on the Trail which now involve shuttling in a car with complex arrangements to drop and pick up along the way. Later they leave the Trail and news of their departure passes quickly through the community: we celebrate their great efforts to realise their ambition and mourn their leaving us, bound for the other side of the world.

Rain falls and mist descends as we head across the Delaware River Bridge into NJ, towards a hostel where we feast on leftover pizza and sleep in bunkrooms heated by an over-active wood-burning stove. The Delaware Park preserves about 40 miles of the river and almost 70,000 acres of land along the river's New Jersey and Pennsylvania shores. At the south end of the park, the river heads east through the Appalachians at the Gap.

The Trail is now above the tree line on occasion and we enjoy views of rural New Jersey, belying the state's industrial and urban image. This surprising idyll is well captured in the Data Book:

Catfish Fire Tower (1,565 feet)
Rattlesnake Spring
Blue Mountain Lakes Road
Buttermilk Falls Trail
Rattlesnake Mountain (1,492 feet) [3]

Fine forest stretches to the horizon, interrupted by lakes and rivers, with a number of attractive if decaying fire towers along the route. Andrew has eased into his hiking and enjoys these final few days with his wayward friend.

Approaching Brink Road Shelter, we unanimously decide we will not be staying here this evening. It is swampy, so mosquitoes are swarming before sunset; a dysfunctional family are arguing around the campfire while their hyperactive dog rushes around in a frenzy; and there is a strange fetid smell in the air as though the geographical and emotional misfortunes of this Slough of Despond are physically expressed. I discover later that Tuk is inside the shelter, wrapped in his sleeping bag and enveloped in clouds of insect-repelling candle-vapour,

---

3 Appalachian Trail Data Book, 2000

unsuccessfully trying to escape mosquitoes and family. We move on quickly after exchanging a few polite words to find a gentle campsite on the side of a mountain where the air is fresh and view tranquil.

We emerge on to NJ23 and call a motel to confirm accommodation. Later that evening a small bar with pool table, jukebox, smokers and only a mild suspicion of newcomers makes up for the lack of good music along the Trail. After the first drink I am home – 'Yes I am from Scotland, yes I have family in the US.' The bar benefits from excellent homemade food put together with care and generosity. The splendid lady owner has a strong arm when serving liquor and a keen eye when beer is running short. The jukebox plays Tom Waits and Stevie Ray Vaughan and I am well fed and drunk in the company of friends as Stevie's Little Wing echoes around. Andrew and I exit the bar with Lynda, refusing a number of lifts and receiving invitations to hurry back. In our drunken state he and I confuse the direction of traffic and think a speeding car will mow us down from behind on our way back to the motel. At this moment however I am going to live for ever and might make it to Katahdin along the way.

Andrew departs for New York and fortunately is not with me when I hike from Pochuck Mountain Shelter towards Vernon. Vernon is a place that sees countless hikers run about distractedly, scream and weep as mosquitoes swarm around them. Later I will meet Al in North Woodstock, New Hampshire, who recalls the spot from his thru-hike twenty years ago. It is a place worthy of the memory: there is a seven-mile hike from shelter to road where the swarm stops and a farm produce warehouse is nearby. I hike those seven miles in less than three hours, covered in repellent and sweat, but nevertheless countless mosquitoes take blood. That night parts of my body are a mass of bites with little skin visible, but I'm reassured I don't need to worry about malaria. I will discover later I may have to worry about West Nile Fever, which catches its first victim in Staten Island. It is a strange thing that places made famous in movies and Bruce Springsteen songs can be at risk from mosquitoes.

Cups of coffee, fresh fruit and sandwiches help ease the discomfort before I hike on with a huge container of insect repellent in my pack. Southbounders suffer from black flies when they start in May and June from Mount Katahdin, leaving most of them with bright red welts across their bodies. Fortunately by the time I arrive in Maine the flies will be gone.

It is difficult to exaggerate the importance of food and alcohol on the Trail, indeed it is impossible. New Jersey and New York remain fixed in my memory for this reason alone, because in those states eating and drinking opportunities multiplied.

The bagels in Fort Montgomery, New York are to die for, although I have to use my very best Sean Connery accent to squeeze a smile from the assistants. I want to sit all day, rather than drag along to a launderette within spitting distance of West Point before heading out across the Hudson and over the mountain to Peekskill.

The multiplicity of choices is confusing. I speak a foreign language when I ask for a cheese salad sandwich: I enunciate slowly, say 'please' and they look at me as if

I am a complete amateur – I must specify bread, content of the salad, type of cheese and dressing, toasted or plain. It's not quite a Japanese tea ceremony, but there are certain routines to be followed and I have yet to grasp them.

I now know there isn't much difference between a sub in the south, a hoagie in New York and a grinder in Maine; all are large sandwiches built with care and stuffed with goodies. Americans do sandwiches in a manner that Europeans have yet to grasp – even in gas stations one can get freshly made-to-order feasts and this is a very fine thing.

With easier access to convenience stores I develop a desire for junk food and am a hound for Chex-mix, Fritos, Doritos, Goldfish, Combos and Baby Ruth's. I eat anything at any time to keep me going. American cheese is awful, industrial rubber irrespective of cost; good bread is as rare as rocking horse shit and later when a 1999 thru hiker stops near Woodstock, Vermont to give us fresh organic bread, it delights hikers for the remainder of the day; and most coffee available from diners and restaurants is worthless sludge. The notion of a balanced, interesting diet and the popular diet of this nation in the twenty-first century are a contradiction in terms.

Robert's earlier description of the Trail food on offer as a choice solely between green and brown sludge gains in truth and notoriety. It becomes more difficult to eat enough food to calm my raging appetite. Others eat inordinate amounts of Power Bars, including Pipeline who has one in his hand at every waking moment and wakes in the night for a top up. Some of us dream of sex and drugs, but Pipeline dreams of Power Bars.

The ultra-liteweight hikers travel with minimum gear and use more and more imaginative means of reducing weight so they can hike farther with less exertion. Their diet differs from others: one eats ramen noodles and salami, Gizmo dry ramen covered with peanut butter, Jack Bivouac dehydrated banana mush followed by scrounged cigarettes. I never see the attractions of such a Spartan existence and my digestive system is in sufficient revolt without any further encouragement.

I have been vegetarian for over twenty years and am used to a diet heavy in fibre; Trail food is not heavy in much so I pay a large price over six months. Digging the obligatory cat hole with a small orange plastic shovel soon becomes a task swiftly accomplished when need is so imminent. Robert gave a presentation to his Rotary Club upon his return to the UK and the slide that got most laughs was one of the orange shovel. When first I waved it in his direction in Virginia, he looked for one moment as though he might do without before quickly coming to his senses.

I don't drink alcohol with a conviction born of long practice or congenital blessing, enjoying instead the occasional beer and malt whisky. The Trail is not for lovers of liquor unless family and friends are busy mailing it illegally to post offices along the way. A number of counties in the south are dry for reasons religious and, some argue, practical, in respect of protecting a trade in illegal corn liquor. There are related activities in the growing of marijuana along the Trail; later I miss a bust in Maine – complete with helicopters, police cars and dogs – by a day. I never taste corn liquor, but know I am dealing with a generational thing when a hiker tells me it is better than malt whisky.

Back at NOC I hitched to a nearby town to buy beer and was not sure about where, when and how we should drink it upon return – we asked permission at the restaurant and yes of course we could bring it in. Lewis negotiated a huge trash bag full of ice in preparation for a long night's session and we managed a few beers before sleep beckoned. At that stage we still thought we could have a normal life while hiking.

I was on the Trail for some two hundred and seventy miles before beer could be bought at a Trail town and a further one hundred and seventy miles before beer could be bought at a restaurant. The beers available were insignificant mouthwash, benefiting only from being cold, wet and fizzy. I travelled by taxi to find malt whisky at one of the state-licensed liquor stores, the only places in a number of counties where liquor is sold. Now with easier access to bars and bottle stores, I drink whenever I wish and discover that some US bourbons are available in plastic bottles, thus reducing the weight of my habit and source of solace.

New Jersey and New York also offer more sophisticated lodgings as I move along through highly developed parts of the Trail. I sleep in an elegant inn for a few days in Peekskill, New York, following my usual routine of eat, sleep, communicate, repair body and gear, resupply. I think about visiting New York City some thirty miles away by train, but can't summon the energy required for this most energetic of cities.

On the Trail, I didn't experience the cities of the East Coast. I sped though Atlanta, so keen was I to start, a city afloat on multi-laned highways partitioned off by huge billboards advertising goods and services available over the Web. I passed by Philadelphia and Baltimore and slept in an air-conditioned apartment rather than revel in the delights of Washington DC.

In Trail towns, I have more time to explore and think about the American way of life.

The Information Superhighway may speed through the minds of politicians, but it is a small, slow path elsewhere in the nation. The distance between easily accessible public e-mail facilities is huge, usually counted in hundreds of miles. There is free access at public libraries, but opening hours and rules of use are perplexing at best – in Peekskill they appear to give preference to young boys playing games.

The public telephone system is so complicated as to confuse most visitors and I struggle with it at every stop along the way, more so in the middle states where there are greater opportunities to phone home. There are a multiplicity of providers, telephone cards that work in some places and not in others, exorbitant charge rates, and helplines with no humans attached to the end of them. Access codes require a systems engineer and an accountant to work them, and a lawyer to settle any dispute. There is an endearing patience on the part of operators who assume directory-enquiry callers know not only the name of the required town but also the state. My knowledge of American geography increases greatly as a result of this experience, gently guided by the ladies on duty.

I try to read as much as possible when in town as a means of keeping up to date with the world. However, newspapers are regionally produced, with city-quality press difficult to find. I usually crave good-quality newspapers and have travelled a long way and paid ridiculous amounts of money across the world for The Economist. On the Trail the effort required to engage with a world outside that defined by a path no more than four feet wide is sometimes too great.

Local newspapers are parochial and report events in other parts of the country as though they belong to a foreign nation. There is a marked divide between North and South, between cities and country, and everywhere a deep ingrained suspicion bordering on contempt for politicians. Politicians from local selectmen to senators are barely tolerated if not despised in a new democracy where universal suffrage is not an old practice. Scepticism and cynicism is the bread and water of the relationship between electors and elected, and prejudice is visceral on occasion in conversation and palpable on paper. And the quality of the writing is execrable.

In Peekskill, Annie joins me for two weeks of Trail experience, fresh from a few days in NYC and fit after months of preparation in her local gym. She is keen to hike, having spent much time reading about and researching the Trail, and been deep in telephone conversations and e-mail exchanges with Andrew and Robert about what awaits her. When thru-hikers hike with friends and loved ones we are mindful our companions are not used to Trail food, sleeping on hard ground, dealing with swarming mosquitoes or coping with rotting privies. There is a new language of hiking to learn, stories to hear and a way of life to experience.

Annie is responsible for cajoling me away from work and into outdoor holidays. Most of the hiking and cycling I have done over the past fifteen years is down to her careful negotiation and planning. Without her, I would still be in London. Without her, I would never have experienced life outdoors.

She is tall and slim with a sparkle in her eye and endlessly fascinated about issues large and small. Her capacity to worry away at detail is matched by my capacity to wing it when we travel together. She talks and I listen, occasionally making a gruff contribution. I think I am interested in life and its meanings, but next to Annie I am an amateur.

A few days later we call into the Shenandoah Tenting Area, which is so beguiling – with cut grass, planted vegetable gardens and elegant camping facilities – that we stop for the day rather than move on after a late lunch. That night a summer storm lashes the campsite: waves of rain strike our tents and lightning illuminates the sky. I am grateful for summer rain because it means streams and rivers are full and the danger of drought is averted; in other years, drought has obliged hikers to travel many extra miles for this most necessary supply.

In Pennsylvania, New Jersey and New York I hike through working-class communities where I see the usual signs of decay – empty factories, closed shops and dejected faces – illustrating the fact that when work dies so too does the community supported by it. I read a book before leaving for the Trail about the long slow death of a furniture factory that sustained generations of local people before being dismantled by a new owner. Closing is a reminder of the power of regular, full-time work, expressed in gut-wrenching words and elegant photos.[4]

One of the many puzzles of the Trail is that hikers give up work and careers for six months. All this in a nation obsessed with work and what it provides, where annual holiday entitlement is low and the safety net for those out of work is minimal. The Trail stories prompt me to muse on what is happening in the world of work – a subject that interests me both professionally and personally.

The work thing is almost as much of an obsession for me as the American thing – I have read around the subject and it puzzles me greatly as I try to understand why it exercises such power, both good and bad. Work soaks up a great deal of time and effort in our lives so deserves consideration.

On the Trail I learned that changes to work in the US are marked even over a generation or two, a relatively short period of time for significant societal change to be accomplished. Fathers no longer find jobs in steel yards for their sons via contacts or union membership, farms no longer pass from generation to generation, and the very idea of a career is changing shape if not disappearing as a number of hikers obliged to take early retirement discover.

I reflect on the difference between my working life and that of my father, who qualified as a painter and decorator and finished his career as the director of a trade

---

[4] Cathy Davidson, Closing: The Life and Death of an American Factory.

company. He used a telephone and telex machine at work where he sold wallpaper and specialist wall finishings. I use a laptop to manage my consulting life from home and participate as a consumer in the 24-hour society whether ordering research material on the Internet, shopping at 2 a.m. or sorting financial affairs at unusual times. Even now, I keep in touch with Trail friends across the Atlantic by e-mail, necessarily unaware of time differences. Technology has changed how I work and relate with others.

Dad worked full time for companies all his life, receiving weekly cash payments and then monthly bank transfers as his career advanced, automatically contributing to company pension schemes. My pension, income tax and sales tax arrangements are greatly complicated by a life that does not fit the norm. I have little idea what I will be doing professionally in six to twelve months so my patterns of work and therefore income are variable over time.

Dad worked from nine to five and planned to go on until he was sixty. The end of jobs for life, a concept taken for granted for much of the last century, is well evidenced in my generation, but not his. The 40:40 model where we work forty hours per week for forty years is gone. When I tasted part-time work at school I shuddered at the prospect of doing the same job all my adult life: one of my father's colleagues, Jean, laughed at the look of shock on my teenage face when she told me she had been working since she was sixteen and would go on until she was sixty-five. In the years ahead this work ethic crept up, embraced and then almost strangled me. I now enjoy a portfolio career where I move in and out of combinations of paid employment, self-employment and travel.

Research evidence about the changing nature of work is supported by my informal and very unscientific findings on the Trail. A greater proportion of the population start work later, having participated in post-school education of some description, and finish their working careers earlier. The end point of a working life may be enforced through lay-offs or redundancy, it may come as a welcome relief following a period made uncomfortable by illness or advancing years, or it may signal recognition that material needs are well satisfied and there is no further reason to work. One hiker delighted in his relief at leaving a job that, in his own words, had strangled him over a long period as his company experimented with a variety of management fads.

However, for those in 'proper' jobs there remains great concern about job security. The evidence to support this is mixed since it is not the case that labour markets are experiencing greater amounts of 'churn', or movement in and out of jobs. It may be that it's a psychological concern rather than a concern borne out by actual experience of redundancy or job change. Nevertheless, even 'proper people' no longer expect a great deal from employers in terms of job security or even career development. One hiker negotiated a career break after many months of effort on his part and intervention by a sympathetic manager, but was still wary of returning to a job that might no longer exist.

This concern about job security may explain why there are so few hikers in their late twenties and early thirties on the Trail. It is too late for them to take the time off they missed taking in their college years and too early to have any freedom of choice; in a very strong sense they cannot afford to hike away from work. The demography of the Trail is interesting in this respect: the highest proportion of hikers is college kids, with mid-lifers and then seniors following behind in terms of absolute numbers. This demographic spread is evidence of a dynamic which may not be changing all that quickly – marriage, children and career still soak up those in their late twenties and early thirties, obliging them to focus on earning money to provide for young families and new responsibilities.

The evidence of any move towards 'downshifting', a deliberate attempt to inject greater balance into one's life away from work and towards other interests and responsibilities, is less quantifiable in both research and on the Trail. However, who in their right minds wants to be 'cash rich and time poor', earn shedloads of money and have no time to do anything with it? I'd rather walk than work, hike than hustle. One hiking companion sold his partnership to hike and celebrate his freedom from an experience that was crushing him; he intends to return on a part-time basis. I suspect a number of hikers are edging towards this conclusion, although some carry huge debts from college. Another quickly calculated that her degree cost $100,000 and she would be in her early thirties before her college loan was paid off after ten years of determined effort.

What then of the move away from manufacturing to services and the increase in service-sector employment?

As one might expect, given an educated, middle-class population, the service sector in the US is alive and well. As providers of work and consumers of services, hikers talk of cleaners, gardeners and nannies. There is a huge increase in service-sector female employment driven by part-time arrangements and a marked increase in domestic help with 'cash rich and time poor' individuals buying in help for their children, dogs, garden, etc. In effect, they outsource household duties to lowly paid domestic workers.

This is the downside to service-sector employment: it means low paid, part-time jobs with reduced employment rights, adults holding down a number of part-time jobs to earn a living and working very long hours for low hourly rates. This multiple job dynamic is very common in the US if my experience is typical, and a number of hikers talk of mind-numbingly long hours in a variety of jobs for minimum wage payments and no proper medical insurance.[5] I enjoy free access to the UK's National Health Service and private cover from my employment should I wish to use it, but am acutely aware that many of my hiking companions are without any cover whatsoever.

What then of college kids on the Trail?

Some have had experience of part-time work in the service sector and a surprising number still live at home. They look forward to periods of unemployment and much greater uncertainty in their working lives than their parents. A lot of them have little idea what they want to do next and the Trail provides a welcome space in which they do not have to worry about these matters. I admire

---

5 Nickel and Dimed by Barbara Ehrenreich describes this particularly well.

their courage in walking away to think before plunging into the world of work, admire their capacity to step away from what is expected of them in a manner I was incapable of doing at such an age. I see uncertainty flicker in their young eyes during conversations on life after the Trail and what it holds for them; on they spiel about doing something different, making changes to society and escaping the bonds experienced by their parents.

Those who are university educated will earn more and progress more quickly. They nevertheless look around and see college friends carrying large levels of personal debt for many years, still having difficulty finding work that is well paid and stimulating.

As such, their careers, if one can use the word in its traditional sense any more, start at a time of great change and uncertainty. It is the case that they expect markedly different things from work compared to earlier generations – a workplace that doesn't contribute to the degradation of the environment, working arrangements which meet their needs in a flexible manner, a work-life balance radically different from that experienced by their parents. A number already plan to work in a manner that meets their needs, talking of travel and wider experiences beyond career and family. For a variety of reasons they will face greater challenges than their parents in terms of skill development: apprenticeships are at an all-time low; vocational-training programmes remain confined to the professions; and skills training in post-school education is patchy in the extreme.

Job seekers can become self-employed and find work in a new market in which employers can buy in skills and knowledge for a fixed period of time and thus make use of a flexible resource that doesn't add to their fixed costs. But the cost of keeping knowledge up to date falls to the self-employed themselves, rather than to their employers, and this is also a very difficult market to break into for inexperienced graduates.

What conclusions do I reach? We can't all be employed in the service sector so growth may be slow, but 'proper' jobs will continue to shrink in number and proportion. The world of work will become ever more individualistic and technological, while legal and fiscal arrangements will continue to lag behind the real world. New forms of working will emerge, but the traditional model has mileage in it yet. The notion of a conventional career will disappear, if it hasn't already done so.

There is a practice when writing about organisations of drawing on a variety of sources – Marxism, evolutionary biology, the life of orchestras and improvised jazz, all are used to good effect. Sometimes it's interesting, shining new light on old methodologies. Other times the strain shows as theories get stretched too far. Like politicians, the writers write of success and forget to mention the sticky, awkward bits and failures, forget to mention that good ideas are easy, but implementation difficult.

As I hike I puzzle too about organisations, my profession in human resources and the relationship between hiking and organisational life. In this experience of hiking for six months what can I learn about selection, motivation, strategy and training? It seems a ridiculous, almost irrelevant question in amongst the hardship and beauty of the Trail. But it's worth exploring in the hours of hiking when my choice is active thought or the riff of a bubble-gum song that refuses to go away.

Others travel a similar path. Osteopaths focus on bodies and how they adapt to carrying heavy packs and sleeping on the ground; doctors speculate about survival and emergency medical techniques away from technological fixes provided by A&E rooms; designers analyse colour, shape and form in the woods. All of us are making connections between old and new lives. It is a perfect opportunity to test and change our assumptions and working practices.

Hiking over 2,100 miles over a variety of terrain and through extremes of weather in a foreign country several thousand miles from home, with little relevant previous experience, isn't life threatening, but could be seriously damaging. If a company were to embark on an enterprise such as sponsoring staff in a round-the-world boat race, candidates would go through a selection process involving strict medicals, psychometric tests, role-plays, presentations and interviews. The successful candidates would then be gathered together for a series of team-building activities and briefings from specialists. The preparation would be substantial and detailed for a number of reasons: the insurance costs of the race going wrong, high risk of early fall out by participants and the danger of the group not working well together.

On the Trail I am entirely self-selected, along with everybody else. I have chosen to ignore what I have been taught and everything I have practised over a long period of time – bloody-minded stubbornness is not much of a qualification for anything apart from being bloody minded and stubborn. Like everybody else I am convinced I will get to Katahdin irrespective of the fact that some three thousand hikers will not.

What drove me to start and complete tells me a great deal about motivation. We all of us move through periods of change or transition in our lives and need to pass through these passages with care and attention in order to grow as a result.[6] The pilgrims or pèlegrins on Le Chemin believe they are building up holy credit by completing the route and worshipping at Santiago de Compostela, and they talk of a 'new life' starting after the pilgrimage finishes. Wealthy believers used to pay others to complete the pilgrimage on their behalf or would ride on horseback. For me, in a conscious sense and in some sense as yet unknown, the Trail is a celebration of an old life and the beginning of a new one, with 2,100 miles acting as the catalyst.

The significance of the Trail transcended all other considerations, the external static that arises inevitably when one is about to jump off the edge towards something new. Before I left London, I wondered why I couldn't be content with a nine-to-five job, mortgage and family. On the train to Gatwick Airport, London in April 2000 these more traditional contentments felt like a comfortable place to be.

My father died at the age of fifty-three in 1989 and this fact hovers over me the closer I get to him in years, setting me off on a route that took me out of corporate life as I realised my span may be as short as his. He

---

[6] Gail Sheehy's Passages may be dated, but it captures this process well.

looked forward to retirement to enjoy the rewards of his labours and never experienced them. So the Trail is part of a process that has been going on for almost eleven years and there is a strong link between hearing of his death and my arrival in Atlanta. I am driven by my search for excitement and meaning outside the parameters of adult family life and traditional definitions of work and career.

I also have a fear of failure and mediocrity.

I am not psychologically attuned to failure and I hate mediocrity in whatever shape I find it. 'Hike your own hike' is a common saying on the Trail, meaning do your own thing and keep out of my face. If it means anything to me, it means get started and get finished. I admire everybody who starts, but I really admire those who finish.

On a more practical point, the Trail has symbolism for me – if I don't make it to Katahdin, I will be reminded of my failed celebration at every birthday until my dying day. I am hopeless at celebrating success, let alone failure, and have a good memory, so there will be no escape from failure. I do not want to crown a significant birthday and a huge challenge with a massive disappointment, all in anticipation of years of decline.

Alongside my drive and obsession, there is some flexibility. I will go home if there is a risk of doing long-term damage to my body or a tragedy requires my presence. As it turns out I will be lucky. Other hikers suffer major setbacks – constant pain, serious injuries and illness occasionally requiring long-term hospitalisation, death of friends and family in tragic circumstances. All of this I escape and never have to compromise my health or my commitment to loved ones.

To manage the challenge presented by the Trail I needed to picture it, but not be crushed by its enormity, to hike and make progress, but not in such a way that the prospect of failure haunted me. At a lovely organic farm, the Blueberry Patch, near Hiawassee, Georgia, where the owners provided a warm welcome and delightful breakfast for hikers, there was a long strip-map on the kitchen wall that indicated the distance covered to date, at that point a miserable sixty-six miles. The 'You are here' was terrifying in its significance and I felt the Trail weighing upon my shoulders, pushing me into the floor. Walking from south to north had a real sense of going uphill, and the hill felt like a muckle one. I needed a means of imagining the hill without it overpowering me, a context in which I could think about the Trail.

To fend off such powerful and discouraging feelings, I make it my habit to focus on the week ahead and plan accordingly for food, water and shelter. I envision Katahdin and look at its photo in my Data Book most days. The miles between the week ahead and the end point I choose not to think about, so great is the gap and distance and effort involved. If I think about this huge gap calculated in months and hundreds of miles, it will push me into a morass of low morale, poor health and bitter spirit.

What does the Trail tell me about life in organisations?

I admire the capacity of hikers for taking collective responsibility in any situation. An injury, some sadness or need for supplies becomes a matter for collective action – can I help by carrying your pack, what about a little treat to lift morale, perhaps this spare bag of dehydrated food? I know if anything goes wrong on my hike there will be people around me, sometimes complete strangers, who will come to my aid with no thought of reward or concern about their own schedules and needs. When Robert's hiking stick broke on his first day, a Trail Angel took it away to be fixed and it was hanging in the Partnership Shelter six days later awaiting our arrival. Communities united by religion, ideology or occupation are like this, but the feeling of collective responsibility can combine with gossip and deep social conservatism. On the Trail it is different, perhaps because the experience is intense and short and we leave it behind when all's done.

Collective responsibility is a phrase I hear often in corporate life, when senior managers and directors talk publicly about their work. They claim that the process used to arrive at a policy decision is informed by research, debate and consultation. Of course, once decisions are taken senior colleagues are obliged to act collectively. Implementation is carried out properly and results are fully evaluated. At all times the board acts collectively and with the interests of the shareholder or stakeholder in mind.

In fact, this is all rubbish. Indeed much of what is said in public about organisations by people employed by them or academics subsidised by them is rubbish. There is nothing better fitted to bear out Hobbes's description of life as 'nasty, brutish and short' than the behaviour of senior management teams. Corporate life is innately selfish and the habit grows with seniority as fiefdoms develop, the organisation resembles a collection of silos under the roof of a name or brand, and a strong sense of politics is valuable.

When next I hear a client spouting the usual rubbish, I shall take them hiking.

There is a charming exercise peddled by gurus in a number of business books of identifying six or seven magical activities that define excellence, creativity, leadership or whatever. Until recently it was a mantra about using the Web and moving at the speed of light, or some such bollocks. I don't know the significance of the numbers six and seven, but the books have a short shelf-life before the next fad comes along or predictions are proved to be nonsense.

Even though it's over fifteen years old, I like the expression 'sticking to the knitting', focusing on what you are good at, because it's right and helps to explain the massive failure of so many mergers. My mother taught me to knit so I think I understand what's being said.

'Knit one, purl one' is hugely simple and complex all at once, particularly if one tries to think and do at the same time. Knitting is about getting on top of the complexity of supposedly simple tasks, learning what it feels like rather than necessarily understanding the meaning, and then doing it without thought. It's about getting the basics right so the sum of the basics looks after itself, without getting in the way of further innovation. And one becomes good at knitting by doing it and not getting distracted by other supposedly similar or complementary activity. Like knitting, one of the joys of hiking is it lends itself to practice and with practice comes comfort and enjoyment once various technical issues are mastered.

When hiking I wax my boots regularly so they repel water and don't need to understand what the wax does to my boots. I treat drinking water with iodine so I'm not laid low for weeks with giardia, the effects of which I fear. I pitch my tent with care to ensure it's waterproof, bug-proof and won't be flooded overnight, but don't need to know about its technical specifications.

I become programmed to perform a series of small tasks that need to be done or else things fall apart. I get the basics right, learning all the time to make small adjustments and anticipating things going wrong, becoming more efficient at the tasks to hand. In the process I build the capacity to deal with new situations. I better anticipate the weather by reading clouds and observing changes in the seasons. I get to know the tiny messages my body sends and respond quickly when a new or slightly different one arrives, possibly an early sign of trouble. I grow more comfortable dealing with wildlife after several encounters, even when I encounter huge moose for the first time.

In a sense, after four months of hiking I am now at home with what is around me and can anticipate what is to come. My life in the woods is no longer so strange or threatening. I belong here and this certainty flows from experience, learning, reflecting and doing.

9
Connecticut & Massachusetts

New England looks and feels different from the Southern States. One key difference lies in how people relate to each other. The presence of money in any significant amount seems to put a distance between people, making them suspicious of strangers as they withdraw into their expensive homes and lifestyles. I get used to people not wanting to make eye contact, to paying exorbitant prices for accommodation and to encountering suspicion.

In Kent there is no public telephone, thanks to an attempt to privatise every possible human requirement. A shopkeeper talks to two tourists about hikers as though we are visitors from outer space. Expensive bakeries charge ridiculous prices for tiny slivers of cheese imported from Europe. A helpful outfitter and an excellent wine shop where the owner knows his malt whiskies save the town for me. Local police behave as though all incomers are criminals and set up road checks for no apparent purpose, swaggering around outside a coffee shop. Not quite material for a Stallone movie, but I know how he felt. This is not a place where difference is welcome, although Bernie and Tuk express their difference in typical fashion one evening having drunk too much, set up their tents on a car park and are washed out overnight by another storm. Annie and I console them with words and coffee as they dry soaked gear and hungover bodies on a glorious day in early August.

At Silver Hill above the Housatonic River and a fine ten-mile hike from Kent lies a campsite with water pump, stone-built patio, covered cooking area, porch swing and privy. As a campsite, it is luxury. As a farmstead, it is a sad reminder of failed effort – elegant walling made from stone hewn and carried for miles stretches across the hill in all directions; a water pump raises water some five hundred feet above the river below; flat, fertile land has been carved from rocky terrain to give a glorious view along the valley. The pump has a long, grinding mechanical voice which echoes across the plateau. Those who lived here before are in the earth, below the water table, protesting their incomprehension.

We swap liquor with Stephen and Susan, out for a week's hiking before returning to their holiday home in Great Barrington. Wyatt and Donny pull in and entertain us with their story of a failed hitchhike home. Wind and rain lash across the campsite, lightning crackles and a skunk steals Wyatt's trash bag in the night.

This campground like so many others in Connecticut is elegant and well maintained, all the work done by volunteers. The Trail captures public imagination, which

A typical three-sided shelter with hikers preparing for the day

finds expression in political acts. Federal and state governments regularly vote significant funds for land acquisition and Trail development – on occasion at the last minute, but always with what appears to be a truly bipartisan approach. The ATC and its myriad contacts understand well the need for public support and the importance of political support, which extends to President Clinton and Vice President Gore attending for volunteer duties. I'm sure they didn't dig a new privy or clean an existing one, but they were present. The Trail counts senior judges and politicians as supporters, many of whom hike. Time will tell if President Bush is prepared to get his hands dirty in a good cause.

Volunteers maintain every single foot of the Trail, even along sections that are inaccessible and fiendishly difficult. Few private-sector organisations can manage a large project with such efficiency and quality of delivery, few public-sector organisations can generate this level of interest and commitment.

Some of the footpaths are a joy to be seen; volunteers regularly work small miracles on terrain that suffers from significant variations in weather and temperature year round – months in turn of snow, mud and baking heat. It is weather that wrecks roads and yet the Trail looks good, even elegant in places.

Work on the Trail is hard, demanding and unpaid, and many volunteers give thousands of hours. Hikers are the harshest critics and Walkin' Home and Diamond Doug regularly comment in registers if they think maintenance or location isn't up to scratch. They believe that volunteers are here to serve the Trail and its users and that voluntary effort should be of the highest standard rather than an excuse for second-rate work.

I see groups of seniors out with chain-saws and strimmers, watch huge wooden benches being built outside shelters, admire sophisticated pulleys to hang food out of the reach of bears and marvel at magnificent and elegant three-storey shelters all built by volunteers willingly giving up vacations in a nation where most people are on a meagre ten days' holiday a year. In Harper's Ferry, West Virginia I thanked a volunteer for giving up his weekend to whack some brush and he replied he couldn't spare weekday time during his working year.

I know of no other example where volunteers achieve so much over such a long period and still retain enthusiasm to come back for more. Sometimes individual volunteers are allocated a mile or two to maintain. Other times work camps of one to two weeks' duration are organised by Trail clubs. I read articles by volunteers and understand how much they do and how much they suffer as a result, all of it with good grace and humour in this splendid cause. Some of them carry little goodies and fruit in their heavy packs to hand out to thru-hikers as they stride past. On one occasion in Virginia I offered to help three seniors struggling with a large log and they kindly but firmly pointed me up the Trail while offering me candy. My task was to hike, not to help.

Descending from Mount Wilcox, Annie and I find a campsite on the site of a Shaker community that survived for generations before a split took some members into the world and left the remainder to pass away over time. The community survived hostility from locals, extremes of weather and the curse of mosquitoes. It's not a hospitable environment at all, so efforts to sustain the community must have been considerable.

She and I stop for the night with Bumble Bee, Papa Smurf the Younger, Jimmy their nephew, and a south-bound hiker. Jimmy is keen to show his relatives they can't quite hack hiking and scorches along the Trail whenever he can, complete with a fine selection of Hawaiian shirts. He has a surfeit of energy and builds a huge fire before retiring for the night, large feet sticking out of his short tent.

At Lee, Annie departs by coach for Boston in preparation for her flight back to London. I wander along Main Street, unsure what to do and uncertain of the next six hundred miles, which will involve both bad weather and a return to the mountains. After a large espresso and a Marlboro, I hitch back to the Trail along US20 in a car full of dogs excited by the smells coming from my pack.

I wander along the Trail and hear a foreign language ahead. Closer, I hear imperatives and repetition – it's a language lesson. Even closer, I realise they are practising Latin. I manage, 'Salve, venuste noster,' to the mother, father (with schoolbook and Bible in hand) and several daughters. I'm unsure if they are animists, early Christians or just obsessive.

A few days later I charge into Cheshire to catch the post office before it closes on a Saturday afternoon only to discover there is no mail for me. Perhaps the possibility of mail was wishful thinking on my part: I am unsure what postal addresses I provided to friends and family. The experience dents my determination and I hike towards Mount Greylock with feelings of loneliness and dejection. This developing pattern of significant peaks and troughs in my physical and psychological health will continue to the very end of the Trail.

On a tree a few miles north of the lovely Bascom Lodge on Mount Greylock hangs a retired USPS post box. In it a hiker, Baltimore Jack, has left a register with a number of questions. The contents of registers along the way are mundane – messages back and forth, a piece of cod philosophy, raging debates on matters irrelevant. I read the occasional one and rarely commit anything to paper. Sometimes however they pick up speed and take off to a place of interest and stimulation. Jack's questions remain with me and I answer them as I move along.

- What's the most useless piece of gear you are carrying? I am travelling light and have shed lots of rubbish. I carry a compass with me and haven't used it once. Another hiker carries condoms in the hope of getting lucky and six hundred miles from the end he may be going home with a full pack.

- What are you carrying with you from home? I carry a postcard bought at Place des Ecritures in Figeac, France. It is of an Egyptian character with what might be a walking stick and a strange hat and is a detail taken from a memorial to the works of Jean François Champollion who deciphered the hieroglyphs on the Rosetta Stone. The character looks as though he is in a state of permanent sexual arousal. Annie and I hiked through Figeac in the summer of 1999 while on Le Chemin. A token of love and hiking past and present, it remains in my wallet rather stained and battered but in one piece. I also carry my passport in case I need to travel home quickly. When I'm travelling I read and touch its pages to remind me of places visited and my capacity to thrive when life feels wobbly.

- What has the Trail taught you? A great deal. But the response that strikes me on a sunny day in late August is about the need for a strong and enduring sense of humour, without which I would be lost on the Trail and in life. In my darkest moments – when wet, cold, miserable or in pain – I laugh like a drain at the ridiculousness of it all. I don't know where this laughter comes from, but am very grateful when it is there for me.

10
Vermont & New Hampshire

The next day I exit Massachusetts and enter Vermont at the southern end of the Long Trail, which I will follow for over a hundred miles, leaving it as it heads north to the Canadian border and I bear north-east towards New Hampshire. The Long Trail travels a further hundred and sixty miles along the entire length of Vermont and a number of thru-hikers will return at a later date to complete their experience of it.

I hike over a number of mountains used by skiers, so there are large resorts to visit with the promise of food, soda and running hot water in restrooms. Stratton Mountain rises to 3,900 feet above a resort with huge car-parking facilities and a number of ski runs scoring the mountain from top to bottom. I travel for free on ski-lifts and experience being off the ground for the first time in months – and a rather strange experience it is as the cable car sways back and forth, empty apart from a few tired and hungry hikers. In the resort, garish ski gear abounds in shops, empty and waiting patiently for the season to start. This is the smart, expensive end of outdoor activity and I feel awkward in a place of high fashion and costly snacks, a place built specifically for an activity that damages the landscape so much.

A recognisable face I last saw in Virginia serves me. We dance around each other in embarrassment as he recounts tales of illness, injury and eventual exit, and we are incapable of looking each other in the eye so much do we feel his disappointment. It is the same farther along in Vermont when I meet a hiker I last saw in the Smokies, arrogantly aggressive as he preened and pranced outside a shelter. He is now quiet and subdued having lost his hiking partner, skipped a large section to miss bad weather and struggled with a damaged ankle. Pain, suffering and experience change us all, on occasion for the better.

Manchester Centre is some five miles from the Trail and is a labyrinth of shopping malls, with stores offering substantial discounts on branded goods. Large coaches disgorge shoppers for a day of single-minded consumption in this symbol of developed capitalism. My purchases include a new waterproof jacket in preparation for the White Mountains farther ahead and a selection of miniature bottles of malt whisky which help me to shake and shimmy on Bank Holiday weekend in August, thinking of London and missing the Notting Hill Carnival.

I walk along the streets of Hanover when Dartmouth College is about to start term. This is what money buys and it buys an expensive education, at a terrifying cost for those of us used to higher education provided by our parents' taxes. And it ensures good, permanent jobs for the privileged few with ever-increasing levels of income over time.

Without rich parents, these kids would not be here. One mantra repeated at school and on the Trail is that the US is a classless society, or at least much less class-ridden than Europe, the UK in particular. But this is not a classless society: rather it is one where the benefits of middle- and upper-class money are very clear. Dartmouth sounds, looks and feels like privileged places of education across the world – there are even braying Hooray Henrys in their identical smart casual clothes and accents honed by private education.

I stay at a Frat house in Hanover. Hilltopper discovers a Scots student is around and is keen to introduce me. As soon as she opens her mouth I know I am on familiar territory: public-school-educated Scottish accent, studying currently at Oxbridge or its type, polishing her résumé with time at Dartmouth. It is not a world I know or seek to know and my excitement at meeting another Scot ebbs away. We come from the same country, but from different worlds.

I collect my thermal gear from the post office in preparation for the White Mountains, mail luxury goods from Andrew to Monson, Maine for my celebration on Katahdin and buy a new pair of hiking boots because the previous pair has finally fallen apart after 1,200 miles. I have a haircut in the hope this will help with the next section. Hanover is the scene of great activity as I gather my resources for the struggle ahead. In the following month I will face a number of challenging obstacles

– difficult climbing at significant heights in the White Mountains, poor weather including rain, snow and ice, and the cumulative effects of hiking over 1,500 exhausting miles. The normal comforts of Trail towns fail to work their magic and good food, rest and clean clothes have no impact on me. During my preparations for this final and most demanding section of the Trail, I realise I am absolutely determined and yet utterly worn out.

The Whites are stunning. For the first time in months I walk above the tree line and it's worth every moment. After a damp overnight stay in a hostel on NH25, I take a stiff climb to the peak of Mount Moosilauke, at over 4,800 feet and engulfed in mist. The mist lifts occasionally to allow views of hikers tucked into nooks and crannies to escape the cold wind and grab some lunch. I enjoy the

Appalachian Trail, White Mountains, New Hampshire

climb and the mountain's rough elegance and strange construction, but photos of me on the peak tell a different story – exhausted, cold and gaunt, my face etched with lines, cheeks shrunken against extremes of weather.

The mountain is busy with yellow blazers, slack-packing their way along this final section, and somehow it doesn't feel right they are celebrating the beauty of the mountains when they have travelled here by car. They appear off and on along the Trail from here to Katahdin.

The descent towards Kinsman Notch is beautiful and treacherous all at once. If I look down, I am safe but miss the glories. If I look up, I am in danger of falling a very long way down a steep and dangerous path. This is the first 'real' mountain for some months, so it takes time for my billy-goat confidence to return. I gingerly pick my way with Lynda and Papa Smurf, helped by carved footholds and chain ladders. That night I sleep in a tent perched on the side of Mount Wolf, anxious that any movement on my part might tip me over the side, but grateful to find a spot, any spot after such a gruelling day.

A late start from Franconia Notch means getting into Garfield Ridge Campsite just as sun sets. It is very pretty and exceptionally cold. This is my first experience of erecting a tent on a tent platform, designed to minimise the impact of regular camping upon the local environment. I wrestle with both this new challenge and my tent before reaching a mildly satisfactory conclusion. By this time, I am cold and shivering – in my efforts to sort the tent, I have forgotten to change into dry clothes and so lose body temperature very quickly. This is a first step towards hypothermia because my body cannot generate enough heat by itself to keep warm. I continue to learn about outdoor life, but the basics of food, warmth and shelter pass me by on occasion if I obsess over an activity.

The next evening Robert and Jaki are waiting in their hired convertible as I stumble off the mountains on to US 302, kindly interrupting their fall vacation to show me a good time. Robert tosses apples, bananas and Baby Ruth candy bars into the back seat. Within an hour I am showered, in relatively clean clothes and sitting in the bar of a fine restaurant near Mount Washington Hotel. The waitress and chef joke and giggle as they struggle with my food preferences and Jaki's allergies. The previous night I froze my ass on Garfield Ridge, while huddling behind my tent cooking another packet of dehydrated food, so I shall make this an experience to remember.

In the Whites the Trail is busy and badly signposted and the huts expensive in the extreme. It's like hiking in Europe where I am crowded out by others also seeking solitude. The Appalachian Mountain Club runs the facilities and the sense of a large commercial operation that has somehow lost sight of its original purpose is palpable.

I also feel myself withdrawing from people and groups and this feeling is with me for the remainder of the Trail. I feel change taking place as my focus and energy turn inwards, away from people and things and towards ideas, which is a new experience for me. I turn inwards to think and reflect and just do not have the energy or desire to deal with the outside world. This may be a function of exhaustion as I protect valuable personal resources or it may be a more fundamental shift.

I hike towards the Lakes of the Clouds hut near the peak of Mount Washington during a blazing red sunset, having departed late from Crawford Notch some 5,000 feet below. A group of thru-hikers helped an injured hiker, a ballet dancer, off the mountain earlier in the day. She will be lucky if she dances again. The climbing is difficult and not without risks from temperamental weather. At the Observatory on the top of Mount Washington is a memorial plaque to those who have died on the mountain, some of whom still lie out there, lost forever. It is a sad reminder of the need to be very careful at such elevations. One hiker was lost in an August snowstorm; others while sliding down the rails of the cog railway line on improvised sledges. The Observatory display proudly proclaims the worst weather in the US. The sun is shining when I enter the Observatory for a second breakfast, but mist drops and wind gathers within an hour.

Near the cog railway descending from Mount Washington, Tuk and Minstrel moon at tourists while drivers fire coal at their bare bums. The drivers have had lots of practice this season, as evidenced by sprinklings of coal dust along the Trail, and come perilously close to striking their pale targets. It is an appropriate way of reminding tourists that we hike this difficult mountain range and they do not, choosing instead the easy way up and down. There are photos of Tuk and Minstrel's bums scattered around the world and I have one of them.

Tuk is one of the few hikers to manage an acceptable imitation of my accent, with stretched vowels, mangled consonants and rolled r's. 'Ahm fair scunnered wi a this hiking.' I will lose sight of him in Maine when he and Nemo meet and his interest in imitation wanes.

I feel as if the wind will pick me up and drop me on US2 many miles below. We pass hikers going in the opposite direction who look as though they are out for a day's shopping. A number wear baseball caps evidencing their contribution to the US armed forces: panting like bronchitic pigs, they have not been keeping up their exercise regimes. The mountain rescue service must tire of rescuing ill-equipped and unfit hikers.

Two academic-looking types wander past complaining about their leader who forces this trail upon them for a few days and is now behind with a sore ankle. He hobbles past later and is good enough to look sheepish. Lynda and I move along a windy, jagged ridge on our way to Pinkham Notch, arriving at night and picking out the rubbled path with torches.

Mount Washington can be seen from miles around, challenging the viewer with its dangerous beauty. Washington is part of a range of mountains called the Presidentials, named after various US presidents. Given the political and symbolic importance of the role, it's a fitting memorial. I feel a sense of disappointment as I hike on, knowing that from here to Katahdin is more or less downhill.

Hiking here is the most difficult, but also the most rewarding – I will return, must return to enjoy this wonder. I am lucky to come through the Whites in good fall weather just as foliage is changing colour in waves of red and gold. The signs of autumn, which will follow me to the end, anticipate my arrival at Katahdin, signalling the finish of a long summer and discreet preparations for a period of rest. Spring must be equally beautiful as the mountains explode into life, celebrating the end of snow.

Maps are very necessary in the Whites because the mountains are dangerous and routes are badly marked and confusing in their multiplicity. Maps represent a great deal to me when available in the Whites and elsewhere. They provide:

- comfort and belonging (I look at a map and know where I am physically, even when I am never all that sure psychologically);
- a means of measuring distance covered and time required to get to a campsite;
- a means of confirming the next town stop so that I can judge my intake of food and savour a little moment of joy along the way;
- reassurance that large towns and cities, therefore my means of escape and return, are never far away;
- a means of measuring how many miles I have put behind me on a cumulative basis.

This is a lot of responsibility for a little piece of printed-paper to carry. Maps hold memory and experience, contain sights and smells, symbolise dreams achieved and dashed. An unexamined life is not worth having and maps help me direct and deepen this process of examination as I pick my way over the terrain of the Trail.

It's difficult to work out where my lifelong desire for difference and challenge comes from. There is no role model in my family, although my mother points to Great-Auntie Kate who was respected for her firm views and assertive behaviour.

On the Trail I am lucky to have my father's long legs and my mother's determination, but that doesn't explain why I hike. At school, those of us in the hill-walking club went into the mountains on the day when Princess Anne was married in an attempt on the part of our teachers to escape the hullabaloo. We returned soaking wet and cold having hiked through snow without proper equipment, but I was hooked. Something must have unhooked me, however, because it was twenty years before I hiked again.

In 1994, a young neighbour Matt needed sponsorship for a trip to Zimbabwe and I accepted an invitation to walk in this good cause (and his offer of free odd-sized boots). I returned to London after a twenty-four-mile hike through the Lake District and something had changed. There was a straight line between this experience and my arrival at Atlanta airport in April 2000.

Hiking is an activity that allows so much. I move along with a riff echoing around my head and I have covered twenty miles. In the Smokies, Otter chattered to me about the variations in birdsong found within the same genus. In Virginia, I wandered along with Urban discussing the theory and practice of the American Constitution.

I focus on the next hill as a target and move the target as I get closer, always stretching the route towards the spot where I plan to finish the day. I walk with an empty mind some days and feel myself becoming part of the Trail, literally disappearing into it. It's a trippy, mildly hallucinogenic feeling, triggered by the release of large amounts of endorphins after significant exercise. I feel it kick in and welcome its arrival, lasting until my energy drains before it's time to stop.

I enjoy this feeling of having an empty mind, of being in a state in which I am troubled by nothing and can exist in silence and peace. It's a calming experience and helps me to view my condition – tired, hungry and sore – at some level of abstraction. Not only am I at a distance from home, I am also at a distance from me and it feels good.

The next step is important as I connect with the soil and move on, ever on. I appreciate the sounds and smells. My senses are alive, in fact my sense of smell has never been more powerful and both my nostrils work together for the first time in my life, so pure is the air. Everything connects – the preparation, little chores and my response to the land surrounding me.

There are other times when nothing connects and I feel a strange dislocation, a detachment from the Trail and people around me. I want to be somewhere else, a place I have to inhabit before I can move on, particularly as the end of the Trail approaches and my energy is lacking.

My days have a pattern. I struggle in the first few hours as my body comes to life and realises there is a long way to go before sleep. I get into the groove and my mind roams over matters unconnected until the need for food and water intervenes. Eventually I stop.

11
Maine

From the New Hampshire-Maine border there are 281 miles to Katahdin. It feels like a hop, skip and a jump away as the means of measuring the Trail reduces to days and hours. The border is a source of confusion, in that New Hampshire appears to finish between ten and fifteen feet before Maine starts. I sip whisky and smoke a cigarette, by this time exhausted. I am smiling in photographs, but it takes effort.

In this magical non-space between two states, where anything is possible because nothing is prohibited, something special is happening. Beyond this point lies Katahdin and the end of the Trail where the red route line on the Maine ATC map stops abruptly and its physical hold upon me finishes. This is the last of thirteen borders so no more can I count states, sometimes puzzling over where one finishes and the next starts, debating the point with others while huddled around maps. No more can I wish away each of the states in an attempt to bring Katahdin closer.

New Hampshire-Maine border with whisky flask

There are no more large cities into which I can escape for a few days.

I must now start counting miles and measure each and every one because I will be done in three to four weeks, after which life will change. I know what this life looks and feels like, but I do not have the slightest idea about the next one. I kid myself that the Trail will help me decide what the future holds, but it will not because such a luxury is unavailable. My new life is and will remain unknown until this one ends. I will take my time to appreciate what is currently on offer because time is running out with every step I take. This state is achingly beautiful and I pause for a moment before I plunge in because what is about to happen will be like nothing else so far. This will be a roller-coaster.

There have been tears, liquor, cigarettes and a pause for quiet reflection at this spot for decades. Low-level merriment in anticipation of the big one. It is a moment of transition from impossible to possible in a forest alive with the presence of all those hikers who have realised at this very juncture that the subject of their dreams is approaching.

The Trail becomes rocky and difficult after the border, slowing progress as the temperature drops and daylight slips away. The side trail to Carlo Col Shelter is difficult but I am flying, in part because I have swallowed too much whisky; I am in danger of crash landing at any moment. Tent platforms appear around the shelter, which is already filling up. This time the tent looks and feels robust as I improvise with tent pegs, boulders and nearby trees.

Sherpa appears from nowhere and I barely recognise him, lumbering towards me with his shaggy beard and long hair. The next visitor is Small World who announces his arrival whistling the tune of the same name. He's in good shape and has grown in stature over the past few months, celebrating walking with Apple once again. We are all of us excited and breathless, giddy at the prospect of finishing.

It's a cold wet night, cushioned by a long lie the next morning. Gizmo pulls in, having slept on the Trail. A number of us leave together heading for Mahoosuc Notch, one mile of huge boulders piled high where snow lies for months. We walk in groups as the end beckons, wanting to celebrate and look after each other.

I have been hearing about the Notch since the beginning and approach with caution. Gary from the Blueberry Patch in Georgia described it as the longest mile on the Trail and took some hours to complete it with his son. There are huge boulders piled and solid for the length of the Notch. Steep cliffs stretch high above and billow out from the valley floor. The Trail is uneven and scattered with tunnels and holes, through which I have to scramble to make progress; on occasion it's impossible to see the sky. There is no snow, but I feel its presence in cold, dank blasts that emerge from below, making me nervous of what is underground and firing my imagination with Tolkein-like fantasies. It is a place of challenge and danger where a fall could result in serious injury. Hand over hand, sometimes dragging packs behind me, I make slow progress. Laughing and giggling, I try difficult routes and impossible climbs only to discover there is an easier and shorter path around a particular boulder. My pack raises my centre of balance and I stumble regularly, unwilling to take off what has become a part of me these past months. Cameras are passed around with abandon because this place is strange and we want to capture its strangeness. I would hate to go through here alone, but I love this climbing and scrabbling.

Whooping and hollering I emerge from the Notch, eager to find a campsite for the night. I lose a camp knife in the river, the equivalent of leaving a legacy. I feel I could lose everything now and still keep going, so far removed am I from worldly goods.

I hear dogs barking through the night. They join us the next morning, four to five lively and friendly hunting dogs with tracking devices wobbling above their heads. We descend towards Grafton Notch together, sometimes assisting the dogs up steep rock faces and down slippery inclines. Pushing a large hunting dog up a rock face by its bum is not a pleasant experience.

At the Notch, the dogs' owner stands with a television contraption in her hands, tracking her investments as they move along. That night the dogs had chased a bear up a tree, which explains a nasty gash across the eye of the eldest dog. In hunting season, the bear would be identified on the screen and then shot by hunters who follow the signal provided by the baying dogs.

These bears are dealt death by hugely powerful rifles supported by sophisticated technology – this is not an equal struggle. And in a nation where obesity is rife, neither is it a struggle to feed the hungry. Hunting just might be a means of controlling the numbers of certain animal populations and therefore avoiding starvation and disease in these populations and the destruction of arable land. I'm not convinced. I am contemptuous of any argument which suggests that killing animals as a sport is part of a tradition which needs to be respected.

I resupplied in Gorham farther back and mailed food ahead to various towns, but failed to take enough for this section. On top of Old Speck it doesn't take long to conclude that eating everything now, right now, in anticipation of a meal in the nearby town of Bethel has much to recommend it. A lady from Devon, England stops to pick up a number of hikers in her minibus. She talks in detail of her love for Maine and her outdoor activities, which allow so much freedom. Her accent waxes and wanes, as her American lilt comes and goes.

Bethel is an exceptionally pretty town with fine buildings and facilities, but it's unclear what sustains life in this place, miles from anywhere. There is logging, of course, some tourism and a hint of seniors with money. The shops are varied and well stocked. I am surprised and enthused by what I see, having assumed that small towns in Maine would be like small towns anywhere.

Hitching back to the Trail along Maine 26 is not easy. The route is indirect and the road quiet so I pick up a number of short lifts, always a harbinger of bad hitching ahead. Throwing up a tent on land near a road is high-risk because it's an easy target for drunks and local landowners. There's a huge barking guard dog on a chain in a farmstead across from where I wait so I keep my thumb in the air. A large cream Volvo swishes past in the other direction, looking slightly out of place, and reappears moments later to offer a lift. The couple have recently hosted Augusto, who has flip- flopped – gone so far north and then travelled to Katahdin by car or coach before heading south to complete the Trail – in an attempt to miss bad weather in Maine. I first saw him in Virginia with his dog, ample reminder that people appear and disappear on the Trail in wondrous ways. The couple recently moved north and are preparing themselves for their first serious winter with some trepidation.

In the back of their luxury car I feel cosseted and comfortable while they talk about an incoming front – Americans use this phrase when weather is about to turn really nasty.

At the Trailhead Roanoke and McGruff are waiting for a lift, so desperate for a pizza they will risk the prospect of sleeping rough near town. Roanoke also needs dog food. Rainbow emerges from the woods looking even skinnier than when last I saw her several states back, having been struck again by a serious stomach disorder. She is cheerful and we spend time catching up with news of other hikers.

We share a campsite that night, aware of the incoming storm. I meet Jack Kerouac, who appears to have walked in most parts of the world with a tiny pack. He walks slowly and deliberately in an effort to conserve energy, so his challenge is to keep his speed down rather than up. In this way he covers huge distances of up to twenty-four miles a day without exhausting himself. His method has a compelling logic and I fall asleep wondering why I hadn't thought about it before.

The storm hits the next day. Coming across Baldpate Mountain in wind, horizontal rain and mist is fun in a perverse kind of way. It is a striking example of how Trail and hikers disappear in bad weather. A number of us get lost while following a well-marked route, admittedly without maps. A number of us separate from companions, fortunately only for short periods of time.

Each day of good weather is to be celebrated. So far I have been lucky – not too much snow and ice in the Smokies, no drought and baking heat over the summer months, and Maine has been kind to its Scottish guest. Today is different.

Long-distance hiking in bad weather demands a single-minded, obsessive focus on the trail, any trail. Weather in the US kills, destroys property and ruins communities. Its range and depth is like nothing I have experienced before. At one moment in Virginia I was sweating like a pig and worrying about dehydration, the next I was in the middle of a lightning storm on top of a ridge and worrying about being fried like a pig as lightning zinged along nearby power lines. I staggered into a shelter less than ten minutes later, completely soaked, and was welcomed by two couples with hot tea and fresh bread. Front Royal, Virginia is at the northern end of the Shenandoahs and has been badly damaged by hurricanes on a number of occasions. The weather needs to be taken seriously.

Hard weather is luck, sometimes good and sometimes bad. When bad luck hits me, it teaches me a number of lessons – or rather, reminds me of past experiences from which I should have learned a great deal. For me, the most important one is that if weather is too hot, too cold or too wet it is exhausting and seriously affects my morale. It is also a reminder that nature is powerful and cannot be resisted – best therefore to come to terms with what the day brings. I ignore physical discomfort and get on with the task of putting one foot in front of the other. There is no other choice apart from stopping or getting off, and these are not choices. There may be no hot showers and clean clothes to look forward to at the end of this day, and there is no guarantee that tomorrow will be any different. I am completely and utterly dependent on the weather, a fact of life that shapes my waking and sleeping moments.

Bad weather is a forceful reminder that nature renews itself in strange and beautiful ways, irrespective of our puny concerns. In the best kind of bad weather, I rise above the discomfort and enjoy the day because the landscape looks, feels and smells different. It is invigorating and refreshing when nature is all around in a manner that is sometimes ugly.

This is an experience few of us enjoy because we no longer work outside and even travel in little boxes; so far have we removed ourselves from the elements sustaining our lives that we see them as hostile and to be avoided. We find so many ways of managing our lives to minimise exposure to extremes of weather and other challenges of nature that we no longer know what it feels like to be out there. We move from house to car, car to office, office to shopping mall and back. It is a sickening progress towards nothing, a life of constant protection guided by an aversion to risk and an appetite for comfort.

On occasion I am so focused on moving along and being 'strong' in the face of the elements that common sense doesn't prevail. This concentration can mask symptoms of hypothermia and exhaustion – indeed one of the warning signs of hypothermia is a stubborn insistence that everything is fine, when patently it is not. Protesting, hypothermic individuals slip into a hinterland from which they have to be rescued by others.

I arrive at Hall Mountain Lean-to wet and cold to find that my pack is almost soaked through, but I find enough dry clothes and sleeping material to see me through the night. The next morning the shock of putting on cold, wet boots and socks as wind whistles around the campsite is unbearable. A few hours later I stop on Moody Mountain looking out from over 2,000 feet to the plains below and dry my gear in the sun. Trees and bushes draped with tents, sleeping bags, liners and clothes make the mountainside resemble an anarchic, colourful steamie, specialising in synthetic materials.

Maine is a state of rivers and ponds where water is in abundance, leaving the impression of land resting on liquid foundations. Nothing is solid and fixed in this landscape; any part may be washed away at any minute.

The necessary fording of rivers provides subject matter for many Trail stories; some suggest that there is not much of a problem, others indicate rivers are dangerous, crossing can be time-consuming and hikers are often forced to sleep next to thundering torrents subsiding after storms. We are approaching Black Brook and I feel slightly nervous, knowing that most of the 'bad' stories have proved to be overstated, but at the same time not convinced. Looking at the depth of the riverbed and the trees ripped from the banks I can see the horror stories may sometimes be true. I skip across, guided by Nomad.

It takes time to reach Bemis Mountain Lean-to as I struggle with cold weather and a slippery trail. Trail time ticks past in different ways, usually speeding along in such a manner that I can hardly follow its progress over days and weeks and am left puzzling over where it has gone. On other occasions it drags by slowly, measuring minute, quarter and hour, and never making haste as I wish the day away. Today my wishes are not granted.

There is a fire burning near the lean-to fuelled by a hyperactive local who scurries around in search of wood. Lots of hikers are on the site, but I feel at a distance from them and can't quite find energy to participate.

In Maine, the Data Book catches the poetry of the Trail in maps that reflect the romance of the area and its social history:

New Tripoli Campsite
The Cliffs
Bear Rocks
Bake Oven Knob Road
Bake Oven Knob (1,560 feet)

Many town names are lifted straight out of the UK and other European countries. I visited Glasgow, Virginia in the absence of an Edinburgh or a Cowdenbeath in which to pay my respects, but Oquossoc is different. I want to visit Oquossoc if only because the name is so intriguing. I just about don't get there when I pronounce it 'Aw-ka-sock' rather than 'Ohh-qwaa-suck', but the young lady in the pick-up truck realises she is dealing with a tongue-tied novice. Fifteen minutes later I arrive in this delightful town some thirty miles from Quebec where, during winter, snowmobilers skate over the Canadian border and back in a day.

It could have been the usual routine of eating, sleeping, restocking and washing clothes. This is different. I sleep in the same bed for three nights in succession, the first time I enjoy such a luxury in over five months. My host in the B&B is Mr McDonald who cooks a huge breakfast every morning and makes coffee so strong it gives me wings. He entertains with tales of fishing and hunting guests, and how he and Mrs McDonald survive winter, and we explore our Scottish heritage. I eat out every evening and allow my stove to rest. Each packed lunch is fresh. Some of my clothes I wash twice. I take at least two showers every day, rather than one every five days. And I don't carry my pack as I hike along the Trail, making me realise how swiftly and elegantly I can move without it. This doesn't stop me from falling, but at least I now fall with grace. I am breaking the rules in all manner of ways, in part because Mr McDonald drops me off in his pick-up truck these three mornings and I return to his place at night. It feels good not only in the breaking, but also in the experiencing.

Emerging on to Maine 17 having walked south from Rangeley, I meet Rainbow and a clutch of hikers – Riddler, whom I last saw on the Blue Ridge Parkway, Virginia, where we walked a thin path between two thunderous storms, and Godfather, whom I last saw in Tennessee. A local man is ferrying them back and forth to grocery stores while enjoying a few beers. As dusk falls he stands somewhat unsteadily in the middle of the road with a fly-fishing rod giving lessons to Rainbow on how to cast. The failing sunlight basks this man in

Rangeley Lakes, Maine

golden colour as he weaves his drunken magic, conjuring memories of A River Runs Through It.

An elderly gentleman offers a lift and insists on dropping me at Mr McDonald's place. Do I have enough food? Is there anything else he can do? On it goes, this kindness and generosity.

The next day I enjoy lunch on Sabbath Day Pond in a canoe that is left on the banks for use by hikers. Sunlight bounces off the surface as I search for moose, often to be seen resting in the shallows in preparation for the forthcoming breeding season.

Although it's dark when I arrive in Stratton it is obvious the town is awash with hikers and there is little accommodation on offer. It is not a good feeling to hike over twenty miles to realise others have driven or hitched and are taking up coveted bunk space. My liberal tolerance disappears on occasions such as these and Nomad's explosions on the subject are splenetic.

Large numbers of hikers exit swiftly the next morning only to return when it storms, piling in to book space for the night or clog the diner. The Bigelow Range is the penultimate long climb, offering views onwards to Katahdin. After two sizeable breakfasts, I set out although it's still cold and damp and struggle across a number of peaks misleading in size and perspective as the mountains taunt me with 180 miles remaining.

My morale lifts when B&B appear, fresh from walking an extra 700 miles south to Katahdin to finish the International Appalachian Trail, which starts in Canada and is not yet complete. They are full of energy and purpose, glad to be enjoying companionship after long months of solitude. Their example pushes me along. I stop and set up camp, mindful of the number of dead trees around. I remember that when sharing a campsite with Bernie in Vermont I was woken at 3.30 a.m. by an almighty crash as a tree fell to the ground, tempted by an opportunity to lie flat after so many years upright. It would be a shame to come this far only to be flattened by a dead tree falling in the night.

From the Bigelows I might be able to see Katahdin. In my excitement I cannot distinguish one peak from the next – I know the mountain has a characteristic shape, but don't know its character as yet. It is out there and that is enough.

I jig along the outlet to Flagstaff Lake, balancing precariously on rotting boards, listening to fishermen on the lake whose conversation carries for miles. I am reminded of a scene in The Godfather Part II, where the elder brother Fredo is assassinated in a small fishing boat as he says his prayers, a measure of how far Michael Corleone has fallen and an act that engulfs him in The Godfather Part III. I don't hear the intonation of prayer from these fishermen as they talk of fish, family and weather, but that doesn't stop my imagination from sparking, ignited by landscape and water which remind me of past experiences.

I hike onwards past Jerome Brook to West Carry Pond, where I fall asleep listening to water lapping at the shore some five feet away. The sound and presence of water is captivating, and it is no coincidence that my best nights are near streams and ponds sparkling and singing on their way, wishing me well in my journey.

After an early breakfast the rush is on to get to the Kennebec River to catch the ferry. The river is wide and deep, fuelled by a dam farther upstream where water is released every day, making the river unpredictable in flow and speed unless one knows the times of release. Posters along the Trail remind hikers of the danger of fording, although some do in the name of adventure or purity of experience. I have been caught before by fast-moving rivers and know that particular feeling of vulnerability when one realises one is no longer in control. The trail descends swiftly before I pop out on to a viewpoint above the Kennebec, which looks deceptively peaceful farther upstream until I see rips powering along.

The ferryman is reading a book on the other bank and I am embarrassed to disturb his enjoyment on such a cold day. He tells me with a shrug of his shoulders that some twelve to sixteen hikers forded earlier in the morning when the water was low.

I skip into Caratunk with Lynda to find the Sterling Inn and the New England Outdoor Centre, owned by her friends Wendy, who will join us on Katahdin, and Matt. Yes we are expected, yes there is accommodation available, would we like lunch? We share a camp lunch with college students recently returned from a white-water rafting trip. They are full of energy and excitement, swapping stories about near misses and the incompetence of their rafting companions. The raft guides look fit and exhausted after a long summer season. Some of the students are ill mannered towards centre staff, demanding extra food and behaving like brats. I suspect it's money talking again and experience a feeling of relief that I never have to deal with the public in my work.

The facilities are excellent, confounding my expectations of a dowdy campsite with limited amenities: hot showers, large comfortable chalets, outdoor Jacuzzis, well-stocked gear shop. This is outdoor life with an elegant edge and I understand why business is so successful.

Later in the day Wendy and another friend Clarkson arrive with dogs, fresh food and goodies. The dogs sniff around smells presented by our packs, returning time and again to work out what it is their noses tell them. Wendy and Clarkson question Lynda about her experiences on the Trail, puzzling as to why their dear friend should be involved in such madness. We trek to a nearby restaurant and club that teems with young people trying to get drunk and older men trying to get lucky. I wake the next morning with a hangover and my plans to start early turn to dust and a day of eating, sleeping and resting.

At Bingham, the lady in Thompson's Diner sings as she delivers an excellent dessert with ice cream before introducing her daughter who also works in this diner. Her daughter is embarrassed, but obviously used to her extrovert and loving mother. Families and seniors eating good food in comfortable surroundings are all around me. I love this feeling of being part of a community rooted in buildings and families, because it's an appealing alternative to my community carrying its roots in a pack. I like carrying everything I need, but there are times when my back is weary. This is my first day off in over six weeks, during which time I have hiked across the most difficult terrain, so this much I have earned. I later mark my day of rest with Ben & Jerry's Phish Food.

Lots of good eating in Maine helps my weakened morale and aching body. The romantic place names of the area – Oquossoc, Rangeley, Stratton, Caratunk, Monson, White House Landing, Millinocket and Bangor – become associated with meals, the names echoing like a US equivalent of the shipping forecast. 'Rangeley, good cooking, fine pizzas; Caratunk, acceptable cooking, fine selection of beers, excellent pies; Monson, excellent eating all round.'

In the diner, I meet two other hikers whom I last saw in Virginia. They have had a difficult few months and are trying to find the energy to complete, supported by watchful parents who are taking them to Boston, cocooned in a large estate car. I wave as the car heads to the highway. Their youthful arrogance of several months past has mutated into something more aware and profound.

Wendy tells me to wear blaze orange on the Trail because it's close to moose-hunting season. I take her advice and drape a blaze-orange bandana over the top of my pack. In a country where drunken or inexperienced hunters sometimes mistake farm animals for game, I cannot afford to be careless.

The poetry of the Trail continues all the way to Monson, the final Trail town:

Boise-Cascade Logging Road
Pleasant Pond Mountain (2,470 feet)
Moxie Bald Mountain (2,629 feet)
Bald Mountain Pond (outlet)
West Branch of the Piscataquis River (ford)

On top of Moxie Bald it's bitterly cold and windy, appropriate weather for a spot of such naked and brutal beauty. This is not a pretty landscape suitable for chocolate-box covers, but it is stunning.

On the Shirley-Blanchard Road, Mr Shaw, a long-term fixture of the Trail with his great good humour, excellent lodgings and characterful driving skills, offers a lift. Lynda and I disappoint him when we reveal we are staying with the Pie Lady, competition in Monson where the facilities for hikers are ever multiplying and thus undermining his monopoly of many years. He jokes about my accent and we jump in.

The new launderette in Monson is so clean I could eat my dinner from the floor and machines so efficient my clothes almost climb out unaided. The new USPS facility is here because of the amount of space required for hiker packages, a forceful reminder of the economic benefits brought by the Trail. Helpful staff deliver boxes of food and treats mailed from hundreds of miles back. I spend time on the Pie Lady's e-mail before she drops me at the 100-mile Wilderness.

The Wilderness starts on Maine 15 with a crumbling sign warning me to take enough food for ten days because of the absence of exit roads and facilities. Given the number of logging roads carrying commercial traffic through the day and night, there are now ways of restocking along the way. It is, however, the very last piece of wilderness to carry me along the Trail.

The weather is glorious as I stride out over ridges, and cross ponds and streams – streams that are more like raging rivers when in full flood. I pause for a moment on the Canadian Pacific Railroad, looking along tracks that disappear in both directions at the horizon. I wait to hear a train and its whistle, but without success.

The mountains are no longer so high; however there is still difficult climbing, particularly descending from a number of peaks where sharp rocks tumble around. The fall colours are at the height of their splendour, delighting my eye with a multitude of tones and shades. It is easy to be distracted by such grandeur laid out in front of me, changing every day, advancing south from where I have come and deepening as I and the season move on. So easy is it to be captivated that I trip on a number of occasions when my head is quite literally in a different space. During diving lessons in Plettenburg Bay, South Africa, I learned that novice scuba divers sometimes forget to breathe, so beautiful are the depths. I took this with a pinch of salt until it happened when dolphins surrounded me. It happens again on the Trail as beauty washes over me time and again.

A number of peaks are shrouded by stunted bushes known as *krumholz*, evidence of the withering effect of snow, heavy wind and freezing temperatures. The bushes are protected from elements in a number of ingenious ways, but are so small they offer little protection to anybody over two feet, a thoroughly inelegant display of twisted bonsais. I pass though swathes of the stuff and emerge on to White Cap Mountain, where wind whips across the peak and almost lifts me away. While the sun is shining, as it has been most days, it remains bitterly cold and I shiver within minutes of stopping. From here I should be able to see Katahdin, but the damn thing is either in hiding or well camouflaged. Its promise, the mere hint of it, is almost too much to bear right now. There are still dues to be paid, work to be done.

I pull into Antlers Campsite a few days too late to enjoy a spaghetti feast, organised by Bill Irwin, a blind man who hiked the Trail some years earlier. There are a number of feasts along the Trail, celebrations of our constant need for food, and I miss them all from Springer onwards. One of my worst meals is at Antlers: a mélange of stale bread and cheese boiled in water with a soup mix on a stove that runs out of fuel before things are done. The glory of the surroundings at this campsite doesn't quite compensate for such unpalatable gruel.

The campsite does however make up for the missed feast. It is on the side of a beautiful pond, surrounded by mountains, with clean tent sites made soft by years

Sunrise on Antlers Campsite, Maine

of leaf mould and footpaths carefully picked out by rocks. I encounter U-turn for the first time in months and I am concerned to see his feet and ankles are still causing him pain. Party Animal is as handsome as ever. Gizmo gets out his photographic gear and scampers around the campfire framing shots with a contraption resembling a huge flattened white sunhat to reflect light, his black sleeping bag a backdrop, and a toy Japanese camera held together by tape. He takes a photograph of me, cooking pot within inches of my mouth, a squint thermal hat over my eye and several days' growth on my chin. It won't be this one that turns me into an international model.

The loons or wild ducks are busy calling to each other, their strange keening noises melding into improvisations of the most bizarre nature, echoing around the mist-covered pond as darkness drops. Thoreau captured the madness of their 'long-drawn unearthly howl' particularly well. We all stay up much later than usual, not wanting this magic to stop, thanking Maine for delivering such glory some fifty miles before the end.

Pemadumcook Lake lies within four miles of Antlers and I charge past a viewpoint on the lake, motivated by food and soda ahead at White House Landing, a fine camp that rests on the opposite bank. Lynda calls me back and through trees I see huge white rocks scattered in the lake before I emerge on to the shore and turn to see Katahdin for the first time, stretching up into the sky before me with waves of colouring trees around its base. This is what I have been anticipating and imagining for months if not years. The mountain rises from nowhere, its lower slopes leaping towards the peak, and I imagine striding along the ridge. The lake is peaceful as if in worship of this beauty before us, against which everything else pales to insignificance.

Mt Katahdin, Maine

I pull the Data Book from my pocket to see the image before me reflected on the cover. It has been in my pocket, carried day after day for months, its greying, shabby pages held together by red duct tape. I sometimes catch a damp musky smell from its pages, so often is it marked by sweat, rain and stream water. This picture has taken me from London via Atlanta to Springer Mountain and then onwards by foot for over 2,100 miles. This picture has kept me afloat when I felt I was drowning in a morass of miles, discomfort and pain. I shed tears of joy before the scene that has beckoned me, and gaze back and forth between what is real and what another passionate admirer has captured on film. In these moments between reality and image, something changes.

Pat from Maine is behind, wondering about the name of a spoof spy thriller I watched on a damp day in New Jersey, lazing in a motel room. I shout True Lies and we giggle to hide our embarrassment in this place of dreams. Pipeline gazes at the mountain knowing that beyond the peak lies a trip home to an active retirement and a new grandchild. Stormy Weather dances around the rocks, camera in hand, freed from the tyranny of her huge pack. Nomad and Campfire look on, happy to be here and content there is nowhere else that feels quite so good.

A gaggle of thru-hikers meanders along towards the Landing to find various messages carved into the logging road, some of them a rude commentary on a couple who travel the Trail in substantial luxury. A klaxon squawks and within minutes a boat is launched from the other side to collect a number of hungry, excited hikers. We open mailboxes, gulp soda and order lunch as I obsessively wax my boots, a task that has taken priority with me since Georgia. I have been forcing wax into every nook and cranny, knowing that this effort will save my feet from rain and snow. Stormy swims in freezing water. The Landing is a stunning spot and we enjoy its comforts. Photos from the day show the strain and discomfort ebbing away from us into the ground below our bare feet. I look younger and happier, content in my strength and capacity. With my hands reeking of wax, I feast on homemade pizza, more soda and Ben and Jerry's. I stock up with fuel and toilet paper before returning across the pond by boat, leaving behind a group intent on serious sleep and good food.

Beyond Wadleigh Stream Lean-to, a selection of girl's clothes is scattered along the Trail. Farther on more clothes and a selection of schoolbooks are laid out on a rock as if in an exhibition. I feel some confusion and concern at this display. Hikers dump gear when they are carrying too much, but this rarely happens on the Trail itself. Gear can fall off when it is being dried over the day on the outside of a pack. Useful gear is often left for the next person along who may be short of a few items. Hikers occasionally leave items in shelters or at campsites by mistake. I work my way through the possible explanations and find them all wanting. I turn to some of the less palatable explanations and my imagination gallops off into the realm of rape and murder. It is difficult to believe crimes of that sort could take place here in the shadow of Katahdin within sight of Namakhanta Lake, but maybe I am too romantic. The prospect chills and frightens me as I climb Nesuntabunt Mountain. I don't call the police from the next Trailhead at Abol Bridge, perhaps because I don't want the reality of life out there to impinge on my experience in here, crime or no crime.

I'm tired and seeking a campsite, hoping there might be one on top of Nesuntabunt. The weather is good, not too cold and the sky clear of clouds, so it should be a tranquil night. I'd like to go on, but it's getting dark and there is a very steep descent from the mountain. I'm in luck and cook supper on a rock plateau looking out over Katahdin as the sun sets and mist sweeps along the valley, creating a floating pathway between the two mountains. This is an unusual experience on the Trail because the vast majority of it runs through forest; the opportunity to sleep on a mountain above the tree line is very welcome.

At 5.30 a.m. the next morning a flaming red sun breaks through the mist; slowly it will burn the pathway out until night draws in once again. Small birds chirp and look expectant, accustomed as they are to hikers sharing this spot and their food with them. I smoke a cigarette thinking of the many peaks I have rested upon when the sun was appearing or disappearing, sharing that twice-daily moment of transition. It's clear to me now that it was with their combination of great beauty and cruelty that mountains captured the imagination of ancient cultures. I am lucky to be here.

I interrupt the twenty-mile hike to Abol Bridge with breakfast on Pollywog Stream and an unexpected meeting with Tex who is heading south. I last saw him resting his tired body in the Whites, New Hampshire. He returned home to deal with a family emergency and then flip-flopped to Katahdin, encouraged by the ever-supportive

Mrs Tex. He's in good humour and demands a photo before stepping along.

On Rainbow Lake a bird of prey drops a chipmunk on Lynda's head as she eats a sandwich. A number of us discuss the symbolism of this act – and the chippy cowers beneath a rock counting his blessings.

Abol Bridge is a place made beautiful by its views over the Penobscot River, but at the same time made miserable by large logging trucks and a small store tainted by the attitude of its owners. This doesn't stop Fenway, Nails, Purple and Dammit from spending most of the day celebrating with beers and snacks. Matt shows us around the town of Millinocket, proud of his home, knowledgeable about its history and active in creating its future. The owner of a local bar hangs from the chimney of his venue, busy with some chore, waving to Matt in defiance of gravity.

Logging is a major employer in the area, but numbers employed are shrinking and will continue to do so. The town can act with imagination and courage or it can watch redundancies happen and its young people leave. I suspect Matt believes there is no choice but to act.

Less than four miles from Abol Bridge along the thundering Penobscot River is Baxter State Park. Of all the treasures on the Trail, this park is possibly the greatest. Governor Baxter couldn't persuade the state to purchase this land in the name of the people, so when he retired he bought the park and gifted the land on the condition it remained undeveloped. It stands as a memorial to the actions of this generous and determined man, who sought to protect the wilds from development and private plunder. There is no electricity, roads are limited, hunting is prohibited, access is controlled and pets are forbidden. I imagine him as a tall stern man with a twinkle in his eye, proud that his gift is now home to the end point of the Trail.

I knock at the office door of Daicey Pond Campground to register and collect a form, which will be my application to the ATC to recognise my completion of the Trail. The ranger is helpful, congratulating me on my achievement and politely persuading a colleague in the booking office to find camping space for me at Katahdin Stream Campground. Leaving the office I hear an overweight man complaining he cannot bring his large jeep into the compound, which is only yards from a car park. Governor Baxter would not approve I feel sure.

On my penultimate day, I walk within feet of three moose cows and a bull, beautiful and ugly all at once. It is a matter of wonder that their huge bodies are supported on such spindly legs – legs capable of carrying them at great speed – and that such small heads can take the weight of such massive racks or antlers. The cows look at me through long eyelashes while resting in reeds, keeping cool and sheltered from bugs, and the bull moans repeatedly. When Wendy drives into the park the next morning a bull canters along in front of her at nearly thirty miles an hour before crashing past some visitors into the forest. During the hunting season, hunters often drive into a forest, blow a horn that imitates the moose call and then blast the moose when they wander into the clearing. These gentle and strange creatures are protected from hunters in Baxter State Park where I hope they remain.

At the final campground a father collects his son who has just completed the Trail and I ask if he's pleased to get him back. With the tact of a diplomat, he replies he's pleased to get the body back, but he's not so sure about the mind. His son smiles awkwardly at this double-edged assessment before he's taken away towards a good meal and a comfortable bed.

There are apple trees in fruit around the tent areas and I cook a few apples after speaking with a hiker from Newcastle, England, when we both take pleasure in the mutual mangling of vowels and consonants. A ranger pulls in to check permits and wish me well for the next day. I can borrow a small daypack from the office and leave my pack behind – I want to take my pack with me, but I'm looking forward to leaping up the mountain. Sleep takes a time to come, and then it is fitful as my body pulls me towards rest while my mind rushes ahead in preparation for tomorrow. I lie awake excited, proud of my achievement and reflecting on what has gone before, and I shiver in anticipation of what is to come.

12
Katahdin

Where is my alarm – I can never find it when it kicks off. It's 5.30am and I can barely see my hand in front of me. My head is spinning because I slept badly. Let's get out of this sleeping bag for the last time. I will be glad when I can sleep in my own bed or any bed for that matter, as long as it's not on the ground. My body aches and I stagger around as I exit my tent, waiting for my leg muscles to relax and warm up. Where are my thermals, where are my shorts? All my clothes stink and I feel sure my hiking socks could walk without me.

I am tired of beating the life out of my sleeping bag so that I can pack it into a sack and it's the worst of all possible things to do before breakfast. I can feel the mountain above me, calling my name as I skip around the campsite. I have come this far and plan to enjoy every minute of the day. I could feel the mountain last night, waiting for us to climb up it in our happiness and delight.

Where is my stove? I could kill for a coffee and some decent food right now. No more dried food after today and no more porridge oats. I can hardly wait. Good food and clean water. I can hardly wait. The toilets round here are first rate – they don't stink like a sewer and there is toilet paper. I couldn't quite find it last night and just about dropped my torch into its depths.

I see Wendy in her car over there. She has been up early this morning to join us on this last stretch. She has brought coffee and muffins and I melt at the prospect of such a meal before our climb.

We are all excited and I can sense the tension around the campground. Gizmo has just appeared from the campsite below and one or two hikers have already departed. They are all keen and ready to hit the big one. One of them is pacing around, looking for his parents who are travelling from the south to accompany him on his big day. It's good of them to travel all this distance, but they had better hurry because he is already anxious. His note for them is polite but boils with frustration.

Katahdin is stunning as the sun rises and the day already feels good. The mountain towers over everything. The air smells clean and fresh and there is perfume from the trees. The sun sparkles and it's magical, simply magical, The stream rushes past, whistling across polished rocks.

I look at the map to prepare for the day ahead and giggle when I see the elevation profile – it's about a straight line apart from a few small bumps and then it takes off like a rocket, the red line soaring skywards in such a fashion that the grid lines have to be changed. And then the red line stops dead at the top of Katahdin at 5 thousand feet and 5 miles. A huge climb and then we have to come back down again. I like the sense of finality represented by the red line stopping at the top, suggesting there's nowhere else to go apart from back or over the edge into a big, gaping hole.

We are all blessed to be in this place of beauty and to have come so far together. I can't quite find the right words to describe how I feel, I am trying to be as composed as possible – it's not an easy climb ahead and people suffer on this mountain. But I am not really in control of my body at all. My heart is racing and is about to burst. My body belongs to a stranger, I feel sure – one minute I am cold, the next minute I am hot. I am happy and I am sad, unsure if I should laugh or cry, suspecting I will likely do both. I want to get it finished but I don't, and I don't know what to do with all these feelings. In this existential hole in which I find myself, I can't quite work out what to do. I am neither here nor there so I am nowhere. It is however a beautiful place to be nowhere.

I feel like a nervous child going to school for the first time.

I think the best thing to do is hike so let's go. Pack the tent for the last time, get the bear bag down from the tree and treat more water. I'll miss all this like a hole in the head when I'm done, but I'll miss it. Make sure my boots are laced properly – they are still looking good after that last waxing. I smooth my thermals down and tidy my socks, keen to be as smart as possible for my forthcoming appointment.

Get my pack into Wendy's jeep, where it's big enough for a game of football in the back.

I'm doing all this just to keep my mind off what is ahead – I can climb a mountain of this size at any time with no effort. I cannot climb this one in the same way because it means that much more to me. It's a symbol that what I have been doing for the past five months is about done. I'll climb the mountain in eight hours but I have been walking towards it since April, so in a way I've been on this approach trail for over two thousand miles.

My thoughts race about, back and forth from childhood to now, across other peaks I have climbed over the years, into other experiences where my heart has been pumping, never quite sure where to stop for the moment.

A small backpack is just fine for the day.

The fresh coffee is hitting the spot and I can feel it speeding me up already.

Gizmo and Greek go on ahead. We follow after applying more sun block and taking photos – Lynda and Wendy look like sisters and both of them better looking than me. Wendy finds the courage to join us on this special day. She can hardly run an outdoor place and not climb Katahdin. A photo of me with her captures my apprehension at finishing – I'm there and not there, trying to smile and not quite succeeding.

The Trail is easy for a while, picked out with rocks and good signposts. Katahdin Stream emerges along the way, the water cold and fast as it powers off the mountain towards myriad ponds down below. Somewhere out there it'll eventually hit the sea before the process of rain and river starts all over again.

The Trail steepens and we're climbing hard over rocks and rubble. I put one foot in front of the other, pushing on, but not too quickly because I don't want this to finish. I want to savour every moment of the day.

While we gather before handholds set in stone, I see a photo and note in a plastic bag. The photo is of a hiker's father on a trail somewhere and he was to join her on this final stretch, but didn't make it as a result of some catastrophe or illness. The words and photo go right through me as I feel the sadness and despair of this poor woman, robbed of her father and friend before the end of her pilgrimage. Her achievement stands to his memory, but this is not enough because he's not here to join in and give thanks. My shoulders tremble as I think about my own dead father and wonder if he is with me now, watching his eldest child struggling up yet another mountain, puzzling about what his boy will do next. I look over the plains below as tears trickle down my face and I sob in his memory.

Above the tree line it gets cold so I add more clothes. The mist is dropping and the peak is now no more. I go hand over foot, scaling boulders and scrabbling over rubble. It's fun and I'm distracted from the peak where there just might not be a view if the mist holds. To come all this way and not see a thing would be very disappointing, particularly when I've heard about the recent excellent weather.

My long legs stretch over the obstacles and my hands grip on to whatever helps in this slow climb, my body working perfectly for this last effort. Wendy forges ahead confident in her level of fitness, through the rocky wilderness of a small plateau, past a group of youngsters out for the day and shrouded in mist. I see their outline in the shadows ahead and hear them muttering as if they are not sure where they are going. I can't work out if they are enjoying themselves: they are too quiet when they should be revelling in their good fortune to be here.

Small alpine plants surround us amidst terrain that is bare and rocky in the extreme; this is a dreich place, made worse by a cold wind that strips warmth quickly. When we stop for water or a snack, we have to move on within minutes or risk chilling. I have the skills to deal with this now, but I want the sun to shine.

Greek charges past us, dressed as though out for a stroll in the park and stopping only for a slug of malt. Gizmo appears out of the mist and we mark his achievement with malt and cake. He has done well to come this far given his injuries and lack of bodyweight. We have bumped into each other since the Shenandoahs so it's fitting we are here together. I have benefited greatly from his advice over many months.

He moves off down the hill into mist and towards sun, preparing him for his trip south. The mist swallows everything in its path, sweeping and billowing over the mountain reminding us in its terrible beauty that this place is dangerous. The park closes in mid-October and after that hikers are on their own – any silly mistakes and they pay the cost of getting out. I've seen photos of this place in October when it is virtually encased in snow and ice.

We move on. Wendy is feeling cold, but still making good progress. Lynda is watchful and concerned for the welfare of her friend, pensive about what lies ahead, almost disappearing into the hood of her waterproof jacket. I am calm, having walked through my nerves, and I can feel the whisky kicking in. My stomach does an occasional reel. Almost there, almost there.

Other thru-hikers stream past us downhill without a word; we don't look like thru-hikers so perhaps they arrogantly assume we're nothing to do with them. Their loss so no whisky for them. It's like that when I meet other people, proper people, and I feel some superiority. Misplaced and arrogant, but I understand where it comes from. We feel we can do anything and don't have to answer to anybody as we move along.

The terrain becomes stranger, bleached shattered rocks stretching into mist, seemingly incapable of supporting life of any description, and yet there are tiny gnarled plants defying the elements. They must be well rooted in rock and what soil is available although this is not a place for growth. It's strange how anything can find sanctuary in this forsaken place where the weather swings across an extreme range. There is a damp foreboding smell to the plateau as though the rocks have absorbed the misery of the weather.

And then there it is. As the mist clears I see the top and get an inkling of what it means to approach this magnificent peak. A large cairn stands upright, supported by rocks left over the years by grateful hikers. The new signpost brings vividly to mind the image of the old one resting in the ATC headquarters, its retirement disturbed by the hands of thru-hikers reaching out to touch. I wandered around it on 4 July, frightened to go anywhere near lest it take my energy, unsure of its meaning at such a distance from its home. Now it is as if the sleeping and waking dreams of hikers are made solid in hard and seasoned wood. It is here where we make contact with those who have been before us. At this very moment when we feel alone in the world, as though nothing and nobody can touch us, we are reminded of others of like mind.

My soul stretches from here to Springer, leaping and jigging over peaks, ponds and towns, mainlined into the Trail. My life has been given meaning and purpose here, my body is part of the rocks below my boots and nothing else matters.

The whisky flows and we share good food saved for the occasion. Andrew's luxury gifts of Laphroaig whisky,

John & Lynda, Mt Katahdin, 12.30, 4 October 2000

rich fruitcake and shortbread have been mailed from Coventry, England to Monson, Maine and are greatly appreciated. We take photos of each other hanging over the sign with the distances to points south engraved upon it. I stand at a distance from the sign looking out over peaks and plains around me in this rugged place – huge rocks, fertile land, acres of trees and countless ponds are all below and spread out around the colossus that is Katahdin. The mountain stands alone in this wilderness, accessible only by a number of difficult routes, and at the end of the hardest of all possible trails it is a worthy conclusion.

I'm awash with so many thoughts and emotions, I can hardly make sense of it all. My life flashes in front of me not because I'm dying, but because there is much to look at with new eyes. My time on the Trail, life so far, friends and loved ones and my time to come in the new life ahead. There is so much and so little to think about and we are all of us caught up in our own thoughts.

Another hiker, whom I last saw in Massachusetts, joins us. He's a large chap who's taken his time along the Trail and stands in shocked silence before the sign, occasionally murmuring a few words. I offer him some malt, we smoke a cigarette together and I take photos of him draping his large body around the sign. He's in a quiet place all on his own so I slip the camera in his pack and leave him.

I meet a couple who are walking various trails together over a period of months as part of their honeymoon. I congratulate them on their imagination and wonder at their sanity, although if their relationship can stand this they will go a long way together. I offer some cake and they offer me a potato. I've been given a lot of things on the Trail, but never a potato. I see they are a couple of great originality.

Other hikers flit past, but I'm no longer in a mood to be sociable. I celebrate this great achievement inwardly, and as I feel both whisky and Trail coursing through me, this much I know:

- I was born lucky;
- my life is a good one;
- life is short and needs celebrating at every moment;
- I can do anything.

I descend from the peak with Lynda and Wendy and slowly we make our way back to the campsite, mist disappearing and temperature rising as we go, and the landscape once again feels comfortable. There is a sense in which it's all done, with nothing left to say or experience. And yet the Trail is beautiful in reverse, the first time I have walked north and then south, reminding me that good routes bear repeating in different directions and seasons. Maine lies below, stretching out past ponds, highways and logging roads. Hikers make their way home across the nation and beyond, while others focus on the very point I have left, keen to finish before snow arrives. The next day hikers finish in glorious sun. A few days later between twelve and eighteen inches of snow are dumped on Katahdin and hikers are shipped into nearby Millinocket until the weather softens. And so it goes, the movement and rhythm of life preparing a way for those who will step out in later years.

That evening I emerge from Matt's restaurant and watch the aurora borealis or northern lights playing out over Katahdin. Although the phenomenon is common in north-east Scotland, this is a new experience for me. Lights swoop across the mountain in huge blocks, illuminating the sky for miles around. Colours change frequently, blending from one to the other in a manner that is both inexplicable and stunning. I stand with mouth open in amazement, arms stretched towards Katahdin in celebration, head craned upwards to catch every precious moment. Hues of red, blue, silver and grey, all shrouded in the dark of night. The quality of light is laser-like, hugely multiplied in power and scope, driven by a manic, psychedelic imagination. Its effect is hallucinogenic, but it is more. There is so much happening it is difficult to follow – I see a pattern developing and it changes as though my efforts to impose order and structure are being mocked – so I follow a trace before it melds into another and I am lost again. I hear a quiet tinkling sound from the skies above as if the fallout from this display is drifting to the ground, but at this moment my senses are full and body exhausted. I am awash with huge amounts of stimuli and don't know what to do with it on my final evening.

I puzzle at the meaning of these lights. Are they a cosmic show for me to worship under? Are they a demonstration of nature's eternal wonders, reminding me I may be finished but others will take my place? Does this experience mark me out, given my friends in Millinocket and others on the Trail will not necessarily see this display? Should I deny this evidence of a spiritual dimension?

I have been asking questions for six months and am tired of forever puzzling and debating. It's time to relax, to accept rather than question, to leave the Trail behind me and go home.

13
Katahdin to Boston

The coach collected me from Bangor and pulled into Boston some five hours later, having successfully navigated the Big Dig, the city's effort to drag its transport infrastructure into the twenty-first century.

The trip was painful and all too much for my bruised and battered body. I couldn't find a comfortable position and my leg muscles locked, obliging me to stretch them regularly; moving around was difficult and yet not moving around impossible. My stomach was in revolt and the toilet reeked of chemicals, so I was squeamish and yet ravenously hungry. I was exhausted, but couldn't find relief in sleep as my mind raced across subjects related and unrelated. My senses were bludgeoned by man-made stimuli markedly different from those to which I had grown accustomed in the woods. Instead of the easy exchanges with strangers in rural areas I encountered urban suspicion and distance, and after six months of travelling at 2 mph with a small numbers of hikers, I now travelled at 50 mph with large numbers of strangers.

The shocking ease of travelling distances in hours that took months by foot offended me as my great efforts were humiliated and discounted by this large noisy machine.

I felt I was drowning in real life.

In my exhaustion, Boston seemed like Dante's Inferno. I looked out over huge construction sites where jagged, arching shapes of half-built man-made structures were ugly beyond imagination, concrete mixers multiplied across the horizon ready to pour their coagulant into the life blood of the city and regiments of construction workers milled around aimlessly at the end of day. It was so very unnatural in form and content that it had an almost toxic effect on me.

The coach station was full of suits making their way home after another long day and snaking queues of patient, well-dressed people waited for coaches to return them to their loved ones. They smelt of stale perfume and after-shave and they looked grey and worn. Rain pattered down and reminded me such places are miserable the world over, infused with a sense of eternal rootlessness as people depart and separate amid the dislocation of contemporary life.

And yet when I summoned enough energy to look upon this place with different eyes, it was not so bad – clean, elegant and well organised, much like the city itself. Already I was struggling to adjust to events around me, reversing out of the changes I had affected some months earlier as I grew used to life in a green tunnel. But it took inordinate effort on that wet day in early October.

In the days that followed I saw little of the city, choosing instead to eat and sleep then eat again. I munched bagels and drank coffee within an hour of a large breakfast. I had very simple needs that demanded satisfaction on an hourly basis and in a strong sense this was recovery time. I had difficulty sleeping inside because my breathing was awkward and my bladder woke me regularly. Normal life was still at a distance: my world was limited to those very same basic physical processes that had troubled me so much on the Trail. I felt this constraint, but did not have enough resilience to recuperate quickly. I learned to be patient as my body took time to heal and acclimatise.

Trail smells had worked their way into my gear and my body and I obsessively washed both on a daily basis, hoping to return them to good order. My gear responded better than my body, which seemed to emit a fusty smell from every pore as though my emotional and physiological confusion was being physically expressed. I returned again and again to washrooms to experience hot running water and flushing toilets, filled with a great delight whenever hot water rushed over my chapped and weathered hands.

My leg muscles were in shock as a result of not hiking fifteen to twenty miles every day with a large pack on my back. I staggered to stand up after stiffening quickly when resting, and had to plan my exit from chairs, identifying handholds before I moved. Walking up or down stairs after sleep was dangerous and I never knew how my legs would respond given they were beyond my control. And so I learned to take one step at a time and rest briefly before the next. Perhaps my legs were acting with perfect rationality and extracting a revenge for everything I had put them through in the previous months. My return to a body shape and means of walking more akin to normal life was a slow and painful process, eased by large amounts of painkillers, conscientious stretching and a substantial osteopathy bill.

My brain was dead and though I now had newspapers, the Web and countless bookshops I did little to engage with the world. I tried to read on a number of occasions and failed after a few paragraphs, struggling to process the information presented to me and find a context for it. I returned to the Data Book from time to time, but even that failed to exercise its magic and my memory only delivered the occasional fleeting glimpse of the Trail. From a shabby Tower Records and an alternative shop nearby I emerged with a miserly number of CDs, thus confounding my expectations of a music feast. I had planned to add countless items to my collection, but I was several thousand miles away from those things that had hitherto provided stimulation and pleasure in my life. I tried hard to shop and failed.

I had arrived in Boston to discover Dick Gaughan had played the previous night and Billy Bragg was playing the night I left. Songs about the land from both these fine musicians had rattled around my head while hiking, but I didn't care about these lost opportunities.

I had worn the same clothes for six months and felt entirely comfortable, but Boston was different and I was awkward in thermal gear, boots and synthetic materials. I wanted to mark my return to civilised life with classic American clothes. On a busy Saturday afternoon I stepped into Brooks Brothers resplendent in my hiking gear, surrounded by smart Bostonians and foreign tourists exercising their credit cards.

A gent in the suit department took a deep breath, possibly literally so because my trail shoes still stank, and fitted me with an elegant suit which was adjusted in time for me to collect before returning to London. I staggered downstairs to buy socks, shirts and boxers that were wrapped with great style and sophistication by a mature lady. I felt some disappointment as my lovely new clothes disappeared into wrapping paper, boxes and bags. I wanted to touch them, breathe in their clean smells and luxuriate in the sensuous joy of shopping. In this very physical celebration of consumerism, I felt the start of my long journey back from the Trail. The exquisite joy of putting on such goods fresh from their wrappers was impossible to exaggerate, but I still wasn't clean enough to be worthy of them.

I bought a pair of black leather shoes in a style that I had previously rejected because it was too contemporary, realising the privations of Trail life had forced me out of my rather conservative dress habits. My feet had changed shape and were now flatter and wider, in part because large hard calluses had formed on both heel and pad. Persuading them into formal leather shoes was not an easy task and I then had to learn again how to walk in shoes rather than boots.

The shift from the discomfort of Trail life to this experience of luxury and full-scale gratification of the senses was shocking. Instead of firing up my stove and sitting on a rock, I lounged in elegant coffee shops surrounded by people sipping expensive lattes and nibbling dainty pastries. I sneaked looks at those around me, wondering exactly what they had been doing these past six months and where their lives had taken them.

It was both strange and wonderful, a forceful reminder of how life can swing from one extreme to the other.

14
London

I arrived in London on a cold wet morning that perfectly matched my mood. At the railway station in the airport's bowels travellers collided with early-morning commuters on platforms which have always been miserable examples of concrete architecture, made unbearable by cold wind blowing through tunnels. The timetable was disrupted and information on the public-address system confused and I felt the dislocation of a jet-lagged traveller. In order to travel, I now had to rely upon faceless organisations and I objected to this loss of freedom and autonomy.

On a train into the city I sat opposite an ex-colleague who had last seen me in suit, shirt and tie and so it took him a while to work out who I was. His day would be as busy as ever and he wouldn't get home until some twelve to fourteen hours later: this could well have been me. The train sped through suburbs and I stared into houses and back gardens. An army was preparing for another day of work, and would soon be flowing once again over London Bridge. My route home was the same one I had travelled some years before when busily engaged with career and professional study. Since then I had travelled an immense distance across the world in both miles and experience, but this gave little comfort. The end of every previous long trip had always left me bewildered, torn between letting go of the past and reconnecting with the present. At the end of this longest of all possible trips, my bewilderment was intense.

The next months passed in a haze of discomfort and pain, confusion and loss.

My long-term love affair with London was at last at an end. I visited friends and while it was good to see them, it was also painful to travel. The speed of movement was hypnotic and terrifying and I constantly overestimated how long journeys would take, accustomed to my Trail speed of two miles per hour. Walking around the city was unpleasant because I could taste the pollution. I was ultra-sensitive to smells and quickly realised that there were few pleasant ones apart from those presented in parks and food shops. I needed a greater amount of personal space than living in a city could provide and felt claustrophobic with too many people and too much urban activity around me. My height, bulk and knowledge of the world didn't protect me and I was very vulnerable, perceiving London as a threat for the first time. I thought often of my experience on Mount Washington when I avoided contact with people and wondered if this was now becoming a defining feature of my life.

My mind was all over the place, but it kept coming back to a question that was literally short and personally huge: were the extremes of the Trail and my success in completing it sufficient to celebrate my fortieth year? In many places along the Trail I had come across mention of the writer Henry Thoreau – in books, quotes from his works and places he had visited. His influence was ubiquitous. At Elmer's in Hot Springs, North Carolina, I found this quote from Walden:

"I went to the woods because I wished to live deliberately, to front only the essential facts of life, and see if I could not learn what it had to teach, and not, when I came to die, discover that I had not lived."

In Thoreau's rejection of progress for its own sake, in his search for an egalitarian model of a good life well lived, in celebration of nature and its wonders lay his importance to political reformers and environmentalists.

I carried the quote on a piece of rain-stained notepaper for a few hundred miles and in my head along the entire Trail. It was the reference to dying without having lived that shook me. I did the Trail to celebrate my fortieth birthday, but Thoreau's words made me realise that it was also an experience that would mark me for life, would remain with me to my very end. Should I at the moment of dying be offered the luxury of reflection, the Trail would loom large on my balance sheet and I knew failure to complete would have haunted me for the rest of my years. Thoreau's decision to break with his comfortable family life made me consider the importance of forcing change and breaking with the status quo in order to make progress. If I had chosen a more measured and consistent life of full-time work with family responsibilities until retirement, I would never have been happy. Thoreau helped me to work through my feelings about my desire for change and my confused ideas about what I must do in order to have a good life.

One winter evening after my return I sat in a wine bar with Sue, a client and friend, surrounded by tired and drunk young lawyers. She was insightful and focused in her questions, helping me to understand what I had gained from the Trail.

Sue wondered if I missed being touched while I was on the Trail. It was a strange question given that thru-hikers were considered the great untouchables of the hiking community, so much did we stink. Seriously though, I don't believe I did miss being touched because I was with tactile people. In the same way that Americans are forthright in their questions, they also tend to be no respecters of personal space. I was never short of kisses, hugs and arms around me from male and female hikers alike and I very much enjoyed this physical contact. In this respect I didn't suffer at all.

More significantly she also asked me what happened to my soul. It took me a while to face up to this question because it was a big one and deserved attention. I wasn't sure what an adequate definition of the soul would amount to and wasn't about to search for it in El Vino's. But I thought I knew what she meant by my soul – it's that bit which soared when released from day-to-day concerns, thought the unthinkable, and was brave and courageous in the face of adversity. It had a touch of magic about it, a sparkle that compensated for the grind and hassle around me, infused normal life and allowed occasional escape.

I had expected the Trail to be a roller-coaster of emotion, with marked peaks and troughs both physical and psychological. It wasn't as 'troughy' as I had feared because I was lucky and the weather kind. It was very 'peaky' given the absence of troughs, but also because the experience was superb: my soul wasn't crushed by grind and discomfort. Instead it soared and whooped on a regular basis, fuelled by all sorts of wonder. To talk of souls soaring is to use a cliché, but I can't find a better way of describing the phenomenon. It did feel as though I was taking off, seeing the world from far above, making connections with past experiences of a similar nature in places mysterious, safe in the knowledge that right here, right now I could do anything. This soaring was a pleasurable jolt out of the pattern of Trail-time towards something magical, a potent mix of exhaustion, excitement and a torrent of stimuli.

In previous trips across the world I wanted to experiment with being alone, given my professional work was so much to do with people and my social network so active. I managed solitude for periods of time, but greatly enjoyed contact with others as long as I could determine whether to stay or go. I wanted contact, but only with people who interested me. On the Trail I wanted to test this some more to determine if I could bear being alone, really alone.

The test revealed that hiking alone, typically through large numbers of people because I was moving more swiftly than the majority, was fine, but it occasionally left me strung out and lonely. This much was clear from my brief journal and occasional letter home. So I sought hiking companions. For such a significant challenge I needed help and support from others; even when I became more confident of my abilities, I was not so psychologically robust as to manage such a monster alone. I needed people around me and benefited from basic human contact with those I respected so long as they reciprocated. Not once did I set up my tent alone and this told me a great deal about my needs and deep-seated fear of nature.

I learned that my desire for adventure and challenge currently knew no bounds, other than the danger of putting myself or anyone else at risk. And I would continue to go out there and push myself beyond my physical and psychological limits. I also learned a great deal about nature and backpacking. I was a receptive student as I observed and occasionally recorded, asked questions and hiked. I needed this stimulation on a regular basis and was pleased my brain remained active. I tried to hike in such a way as to leave no trace – collected trash and packed it out, refused to light campfires, always chose a campsite carefully and tidied around the next morning. My respect for nature, which had been with me since boyhood, had become stronger than ever before and I needed to reaffirm it regularly. Indeed, my respect occasionally shaded into wonder and worship, and this state of reverence will remain with me irrespective of how much I know, really know, about nature. I'm with Thoreau on this: knowledge need not sweep wonder away, but it can deepen and strengthen the experience.

I started, struggled and finished and along the way met wonderful people, saw wonderful things and learned much. Never before had I truly experienced freedom and space. To do it all in a six-month period was a significant achievement and one that filled me with pride and humility. Pride for obvious reasons, fuelled I'm sure by a certain sense of joining an élite, and humility because I was very lucky to have this entire experience. Without an abundance of luck, I would have failed.

I went to the woods to celebrate, experience a serious challenge and take time out from a balanced life. The celebration, although perhaps a perverse one, was complete and whole. Nobody or nothing can take it away from me, reduce its significance or gainsay its value. It was as good a celebration as any other I can imagine.

Provisionally, I reached the conclusion that the Trail had been a success, but I felt that such a conclusion was insufficient to capture the complexity of hiking over 2,100 miles at such a keen moment in my life. It was too early to arrive at a meaningful understanding of my experience. The real truth will emerge over long years rather than short months.

The Trail also obliged me to consider other aspects of my life, prompted in part by a question thrown at me when I was in a launderette somewhere in New England: wasn't this travel thing just a smokescreen obscuring bigger issues? I had been asked this question before and the motivation behind it always puzzled me because it assumed so much:

- a more conventional life allows one to deal with bigger issues and so dispel the occasional smokescreen or distraction created by many of us;

- one can't deal with bigger issues while travelling;
- a good life has to be consistent over time, activity and location and doesn't allow for wilful disruption;
- age brings with it an imperative to settle and certain responsibilities in respect of family, relationships and property;
- distractions are necessarily a bad thing as a means of dealing with change.

I have seen very little evidence to support any of these assumptions.

Nevertheless, as I struggled to engage with my old life the question remained with me. If the Trail was to mark a transition from my first forty years to the rest of my life, I needed to acknowledge a number of issues:

- I loved the wilds, but cities attracted me more because of the sheer variety offered, although I would have to work hard on my new relationship with London. The wilds of the US or even the countryside of the UK were not for me because I couldn't bear being alone for long periods of time;
- I wanted to move to another country, probably far away because I now relished the weirdness of life outside Europe. It was time to work on another continent, to travel, but then to stop for a few years. I had spent forty years in the UK and that was enough;

- I wanted to return to full-time employment and apply my professional skills within a single organisation rather than consult with a number. I wanted to be intimately involved in one organisation and so confront difficult and challenging circumstances over time. After three years' consulting and six months' hiking, I needed to engage once again;
- I increasingly valued solitude as a means of repairing and recuperating;
- I continued to value excitement and adventure.

This looked and felt like a suitable if somewhat paradoxical manifesto.

As I assimilated my experience of the Trail, I struggled to understand things American. For all my reading and study and my observation over six months travelling through East Bumfuck, I remained puzzled by this complex nation. The issues that troubled me as a teenage boy in Cowdenbeath troubled me again as an adult man in London. The country was just too big, too overpowering and I had too limited an overview to draw any meaningful conclusions. But to believe that was an easy way out and ignored the challenge inherent in trying to understand this beautiful beast.[7]

I arrived with a series of contradictory pictures of the nation, informed by my interest in politics and culture. After six months and 2,100 miles these contradictions remained in place, and were to some

---

[7] It would have been easier to read Harry Evans's The American Century.

extent more profound across divides of wealth, race, class and popular culture.

The 2000 election provided a stark picture of a nation divided – and yet these divisions did not prove unbridgeable. In part this was testimony to the nation's capacity for moving along and getting on with life, irrespective of doubt or impropriety. Bush was President, Gore was Forgotten, Hillary was playing a long game and Clinton was history, although he took time to learn this lesson. I found it difficult to imagine any other democratic country where the seas would close so easily over such a brutal election.

This was a nation where the deal was all-important and compromise elevated to an art, sweeping principle and conviction before it. It was in this capacity to resist memory and deny the true import of history that Gore Vidal found the place he called 'Amnesia'. In a country where tradition is worshipped and regularly reinvented, this loss of political memory was truly shocking. Little wonder politicians are held in such contempt. Little wonder people get the politicians they deserve.

I left the country with a knowledge and respect for its industrial and agricultural heritage, in part because this experience taught me much that was new. I had somehow assumed the nation moved from agriculture through industrialisation to a service economy with little pain and little damage. How wrong I was. Those involved in creating this heritage have struggled over decades in desperately difficult circumstances to wrench a living from the land or that which the land provided.

I admired this determination and aptitude for hard punishing work, the willingness to do whatever was necessary to make a life and support one's family. Mindful of the contradictions of the American Dream, I greatly admired this capacity for believing one was capable of advancement through hard work and application. The songs celebrating the US work ethic were easy to appreciate for a Scot steeped in a similar music.

The insularity of the nation is well documented and evident to anybody who cares to look. What surprised me was the warmth of welcome afforded to strangers and the absolute lack of reserve in social situations. It was a new and sometimes disarming experience, but I grew used to it over time and realised how much it buoyed me. People saw I was paying my dues and responded with great generosity and good humour, particularly in the South. For this I was very grateful.

Within this insularity there was also an admirable independence of thought and action. As a buttoned-up Scot I found the willingness to do what one wanted because one wanted to do it refreshing. I have learned from this and look forward to practising a more direct way of living. No more dancing around the handbags for me.

What captured my heart and will remain with me for ever was the land with its wide, open spaces and natural beauty. It is almost impossible to describe without spiralling off in torrents of over-used adjectives or well-worn clichés. Suffice it to say that when I look at photos, dip into the Data Book or remember certain experiences, I am transfixed and know I must return. The land is stunning and its hold over me continues; I am beguiled by its beauty. I grew up in a busy country, on a small island covered by roads, villages and cities. The US is different and its difference speaks to me in a new and powerful voice.

My physical journey along the Trail has ended, but my intellectual and psychological exploration of things American continues.

Photographs & Maps

Front cover photo	Robert Martin & Jon Bilous, Shutterstock
Appalachian Trail Map	Appalachian Trail Conservancy
p 18/19	Appalachian Trail Conservancy
p 33	Robert Martin
p 82/83	Robert Martin
p 86	Robert Martin
p 96	Lynda Holich
p 115	Lynda Holich
p 148	Annie Williams
p 157	Jaminnbenji, Shutterstock
p 166	Lynda Holich
p 177	Lynda Holich
p 185	Lynda Holich
p 186	Stephen G Page, Shutterstock
p 200	Wendy Polstein
p 224	Glenn Reynolds

When John is not hiking, running, swimming and cycling, he is a mediator, www.abune.org. John welcomes feedback and comments on this book – john@abune.org

Printed in Great Britain
by Amazon